PRAISE

"One of the things I love about these books is that they are so accessible to every aspiring writer."

— RICK LUDWIG, AUTHOR OF *MIRRORED*

"I reread these books before I start each book I write."

— CALLIE HUTTON, *USA TODAY*-BESTSELLING
AUTHOR OF *FOR THE LOVE OF THE VISCOUNT*

"Bernhardt shows you exactly what makes literary characters keep people interested and how to use those strengths when creating characters of your own."

— R.J. JOHNSON, AUTHOR OF *THE TWELVE STONES*

"Easy to read while delivering good material with some occasional humor."

— DAVID SULLIVAN, AUTHOR

"This book gives everything that it promises. And all the other writing books written by William Bernhardt are on my wish list."

— C.H. SCARLETT, AUTHOR

EXCELLENT EDITING

The Writing Process

WILLIAM BERNHARDT

BABYLON
BOOKS

Dedicated to all the Red Sneaker Writers
You cannot fail if you refuse to quit.

"What is written without effort is generally read without pleasure."

— SAMUEL JOHNSON

INTRODUCTION

If this is not your first Red Sneaker book, or if you've attended Red Sneaker retreats or conventions, you can skip to Chapter One. If you're new, let me take a moment to explain.

I've been telling stories for several decades, doing almost every kind of writing imaginable. I've been speaking at workshops and conferences almost as long. Every time I step behind the podium I see long rows of talented people frustrated by the fact that they haven't sold any books. Yes, the market is changing and agents are hard to find and self-publishing can be challenging. But when aspiring writers work hard but still don't succeed…there's usually a reason. Too often enormous potential is lost due to a lack of fundamental knowledge. Sometimes a little guidance is all that stands between an unknown writer and a satisfying writing career.

I've seen writing instructors and writing texts that seem more interested in appearing literary than in providing useful information. Sometimes I think presenters do more to obfuscate the subject than to explain it. Perhaps they feel that if they make the writing process as mysterious as possible, it will make them seem profound—or perhaps they don't understand the subject well themselves. Some of the best writers I know are not particularly good teachers, because they've never thought consciously about the creative process.

Hoping to be more useful, I founded the Red Sneaker Writing Center. Why Red Sneakers? Because I love my red sneakers. They're practical, flexible, sturdy—full of flair and fun. In other words, they're exactly what writing instruction should be. Practical, dynamic, and designed to unleash the creative spirit, to give the imagination a platform for creating wondrous work.

I held the first Red Sneaker Writers conference in 2005. I invited the best speakers I knew, people who had published many books but also could teach. Then I launched my small-group writing retreats—intensive days working with a handful of aspiring writers. The retreats gave me the opportunity to read, edit, and work one-on-one with people so I could target their needs and make sure they got what would help them most. This approach worked well and I'm proud to say a substantial number of writers have graduated from my programs, published, and even hit the bestseller lists. But of course, not everyone can attend a retreat.

This book, and the other in this series, are designed to provide assistance to writers regardless of their location. The books are short, inexpensive, and targeted to specific areas where a writer might want help.

Let me see if I can anticipate your questions:

Why are these books so short? Because I've expunged the unnecessary and the unhelpful. I've pared it down to the essential information, useful ideas that can improve the quality of your writing. Too many instructional books are padded with excerpts and repetition to fill word counts required by book contracts. That's not the Red Sneaker way.

Why are you writing several different books instead of one big book? I encourage writers to commit to writing every day and to maintain a consistent writing schedule. Sometimes reading about writing can be an excuse for not writing. You can read the Red Sneaker books without losing much time. In fact, each can be read in an afternoon. Take one day off from your writing. Make notes as you read. See if that doesn't trigger ideas about how you might improve your writing. Then get back to work.

You reference other books as examples, but you rarely quote excerpts. Why?

Two reasons. First, I'm trying to keep these books brief. I will cite a book as an example, and if you want to look up a particular passage, it's easy enough to do. You don't need me to cut and paste it for you. Second, if I quote from materials currently under copyright protection, I have to pay a fee, which means I'd need to raise the price of the book. I don't want to do that. I think you can grasp my points without reading copyrighted excerpts. Too often, in my opinion, excessive excerpting is done to pad the page count.

Why does each chapter end with exercises?

The exercises are a completely integrated and essential part of the book, designed to simulate what happens in my small-group writing retreats. Samuel Johnson was correct when he wrote: *Scribendo disces scribere*. Meaning: You learn to write by writing. These principles won't be concretized in your brain until you put them into practice.

So get the full benefit from this book. Complete the exercises. If you were in one of my retreats, this would be your homework. I won't be hovering over your shoulder as you read this book— but you should do the exercises anyway.

What else does the Red Sneaker Writers Center do?

We send out a free e-newsletter filled with writing advice, market analysis, and other items of interest. If you would like to be added to the mailing list, please visit my website. We also have a free bi-weekly Red Sneaker podcast with all the latest news and interviews with industry professionals. I host an annual conference, WriterCon, over Labor Day weekend and small-group writing retreats throughout the year. There will be future books in this series. And we sponsor a literary magazine called *Conclave* that would love to see you submit your poems, short fiction, and creative nonfiction. Our Balkan Press publishes books, primarily fiction and poetry.

Okay, enough of the warm-up act. Read this book. Then write your story. Follow your dreams. Never give up.

William Bernhardt

WRITING IS A PROCESS

"My pencils outlast the erasers."

— VLADIMIR NABOKOV

For most people, writing their first book takes a good long time—and finding a publisher for that book takes even longer. Granted, the advent of eBooks and viable self-publishing alternatives have streamlined the waiting game for some, but for most, especially those in traditional publishing, writing is a time-consuming process. I frequently hear aspiring writers complain about how long it takes to finish a book, and then, after a brief pause, they lean into my ear and whisper, "Can you give me a shortcut? How do you do it?"

I suppose since I've written over forty books they think I must have some magic trick, an enchanted word processor or something. If they knew how long I've been at it, or how many hours a day I put into it, they wouldn't bother asking. But since they do, I always give the same reply.

"There are no shortcuts. Sit down and write."

The other pattern I've noticed, far too frequently, is that after writers have finally broken through, published that first book, had a little success—they think it's going to be easy from now on. A little validation can go a long way, I suppose. And this leads to what is commonly known as the Sophomore Book Problem. Put bluntly: The second book is rarely as good as the first. Why? Because the writer either thinks they're a proven genius or this is a snap so they crank some silly thing out too quickly without taking it through all the steps of the writing process.

My first book, *Primary Justice*, got me a three-book contract. Having now had a tiny taste of success, I plowed into the sequel, writing quickly and basically amusing myself with little thought to my audience. To be fair, I was practicing law full-time and had a baby at home, but those are not excuses for mediocre work. My saving grace was that I had a wonderful editor, Joe Blades, who wouldn't let me commit writer-suicide. "This isn't as good," he told me bluntly. He marked up the manuscript till it dripped with blood-red ink, gave me extensive notes—and six weeks to make it better. Otherwise, he wasn't publishing it.

Hardest six weeks of my life. But I got it done. Opinions differ on whether my second book is as good as the first, but at least it wasn't a complete embarrassment. And Joe taught me a lesson that has stuck with me to this day. No matter how smart I think I am, no matter how brilliant the premise is, there are no short-cuts. Writing a book takes time. Period. If you don't have the time, you're in the wrong field.

Writing is a process with no shortcuts that will not jeopardize the quality of your work.

EFFICIENCY IS NOT SLACKING

THAT SAID, I CAN GIVE YOU SOME SUGGESTIONS ON HOW TO produce a first-rate book, not quickly, but without wasting time unnecessarily. As you read the subsequent chapters, you may think to yourself, Holy smokes! This writing process stuff would take forever! And the truth is, the first time you implement this plan, the first time you work through all the steps, it may take a long time. So what? If book writing were easy, everyone would be doing it. Imagine a world in which everyone who ever wanted to write a book actually did. There would be so many novels no one would know what to read next.

Writing is hard.

There are no miracle drugs, miracle devices, or miracle software programs that will make you a brilliant writer. If you're thinking drink or drugs will put you on the fast track to genius, think again. No one ever wrote anything worth reading under the influence, and any stories you've heard to the contrary are probably apocryphal. Or perhaps you've heard there's a magic formula for writing genre fiction. There isn't. You can buy all the fancy laptops and toys your heart desires, if you can afford them. But writing will still be hard.

But—here's the secret. Every time you implement the writing process, each time you work through the steps, it will get a little easier. And eventually, you will realize that you do in fact save time, because you spend fewer hours staring out the window ruminating, or trying to figure out what happens next, or trashing complete drafts because you omitted something critical. The writing process will give you the means to produce a book without sacrificing quality or wasting time. Isn't that what you want?

Some readers may be surprised that a book with "Editing" in the title actually covers the entire writing process, from inception to finish. Isn't editing something you do after it's done, or at least after the first draft is completed? My answer is a resounding no. Editing is not the same as revising or proofreading. Editing is an ongoing process pertaining to every step, first draft to last. I will cover post-draft revision, but this book will include much more.

Kurt Vonnegut said every writer has about a million words of garbage they have to write before they get to the good stuff. Probably true. Malcolm Gladwell says you need to put in 10,000 hours before you can be a first-rate anything (*Outliers*). There is no substitute for the investment of time preparing yourself to be a published writer, which has two steps. The first step will be time spent reading, writing, and listening. Not talking. Listening. Not performing. Watching. Thinking about your ideas and developing them. And the second step, of course, will be time spent practicing your craft, which means putting your fingers on the keyboard and working. That's what writers do.

Even after you get good at it, it will still be hard work. I *can* give you a strategy for getting the work done efficiently and effectively. But it will never be easy.

Seven Habits of Highly Effective Writers

I am always amazed when people ask about my daily routine —when do I start writing, where do I write, how long do I write each day, etc. Who cares? Writers need to develop their own routine. Hugo and Hemingway apparently wrote standing up, and they were fine writers, but you're never going to catch me doing that. Georges Simenon and Douglas Trumbo apparently wrote in the bathtub, but sorry, I paid too much for my MacBook. What you need is a routine that works for you and doesn't become an excuse to waste time or not actually write.

I typically get up early and start writing. In my experience, most productive writers are morning people, though not all. There are some who mess around in the morning and start in the afternoon, and there are even some night owls who write all night long and sleep late into the day. My brain works best in the morning so that's when I write. Once I'm in the zone, I'm completely focused. I don't know what's going on around me and typically don't even look up. After a scene is completed, I might note the time, and I'm often astounded by how many hours have passed. That's what the psychiatric world calls "flow." Time passes without notice. You're in another place. You're getting your work done.

My ability to block out the world was hard-won, mostly developed during the early years when I didn't have the luxury of only writing when all the circumstances were perfect. I was busy. So I wrote in cars, airplanes, shopping malls. I've written in hospitals and playgrounds. I was grateful that writing allowed me to be at home when my children were growing up, but "Be quiet, Daddy's working" was more a joke than a rule. I had to learn to block out everything else and focus on my work. So I did.

Typically, writers work somewhere around five to six hours a day, depending upon how well the words are flowing and how close they are to finishing. I'm not saying it's not possible to work longer, but at some point the brain becomes fatigued and you're not doing your best work. That's when it's time to do something else—work your other job, or pay the bills, or manage your investments, or cook dinner, or walk around the block. Most writers have second jobs, not only for the additional income but because it provides social contacts that might fuel future stories. Many writers teach, a profession that often appeals to the same intellectual instincts that lead to writing. People complain about what professors are paid, but the truth is, professors are paid in two ways. They receive money, which is…adequate, but more importantly, they are paid in time. The job often leaves enough time to get some writing done, at least during the summer. Any job that allows you to do that is a precious gift. But whether your job permits it or not, you must find a way to write on a regular schedule. True writers will find a way. That perseverance, that determination, is the single most important quality of successful writers. That's why it's the first thing I say in every one of these Red Sneaker books.

1) **Never give up.**
   Here are the other essential guidelines:
   2) **Don't wait too long to start.**
   3) **Don't start writing before thinking.**
   4) **Don't stop writing when it's "good enough."**
   5) **Don't allow your writing to be compromised by errors.**
   6) **Don't be afraid to try something new or different.**
   7) **Don't lose confidence in yourself or your work.**

Perhaps because most fiction writers have a college education behind them, they tend to wait until the last possible moment to start writing. After all, that worked well enough in college, right? You procrastinated, preoccupied by your busy schedule of keggers and all-night Risk games, and didn't get started on that Comp 2 essay until it was due the next day. So you pulled an all-nighter, fueled by youthful exuberance, caffeine, and Adderall, and managed to produce a reasonably decent paper. Probably not your best work. But you graduated.

That won't cut it in the world of fiction.

For starters, there's far too much competition. "Good enough" will never get you published. All those romantic stories you heard in English class about poets and authors finishing great works in a crazed rush of brilliance are probably false. Authors love to tell those stories because it suggests some sort of mad genius, but that doesn't make them true. For years, Robert Frost said that his favorite poem, "Stopping by Woods on a Snowy Evening," was composed all at once in a sudden burst of inspiration. The problem is, the original draft has been discovered in his papers, and it appears to have been extensively revised over time.

Don't confuse storytelling with reality. Writing is time-consuming, and if you wait too late too to start, you will not do your best work. A mediocre effort is unlikely to push you to the ranks of the published. Creating something publishable is the result of a protracted, sustained effort, not a rapid burst of brilliance.

The fear of standing out, of being different from the pack, isn't limited to writing, much less fiction writing. In most professions, conformity is more pervasive than originality. Physicians tend to dress alike and have interchangeable offices. Lawyers tend to use the same archaic language that makes their documents incomprehensible. Imitation is less demanding than originality, and safer.

It is also the kiss of death when you're trying to get published, and I want to discuss this here, because part of the writing process should be devoted to rooting out imitation and replacing it with originality. In my earlier book *Promising Premise*, I discussed the concept of "the same, but different." Appealing premises often fall into a recognizable genre, but they will also have something different, some inversion of expectation or divergence from the norm that spurs reader interest. Some element of originality is crucial to grabbing a larger audience, whether you seek a popular audience or a literary one. The largest rewards go, not to the wolves that run with the pack, but to the wolves that explore uncharted territory.

This need for originality has become more important than ever with the rise of eBooks and self-publishing. The greatest eBook sales have been for adult genre fiction, meaning romance-erotica, science fiction-fantasy, and mystery-thriller-suspense. Too often, self-published authors focus on complying with genre conventions, often in the most predictable ways, and then compensating for mediocrity with low prices and extensive social media promotion. I suppose that is a sort of success, but my goal is to teach people how to write well. Formulaic writing that appeals to undemanding bargain shoppers is not what will distinguish you. Originality will.

Of course, every time you try something different, you're taking a risk. Failure is always a possibility, and no one, not even the most brilliant writers, hit a home run every time. To the contrary, every writer you admire and love had some failures. Some books are better than others. Some withstand the test of time and others do not. Despite my success with the Ben Kincaid series, I always pushed to publish other books outside the series, and frankly, some of those are better than others. No regrets. You never know what's going to happen until you try. If you give it your best effort, with a lot of concentrated hard work, there's no need for shame. Win or lose, you tried. And I have to note that, in the world of literature, it is hardly unusual for trailblazing work to be largely unappreciated in the author's lifetime. Particularly with the outliers, Dickinson, Whitman, Melville, Woolf, and many others, it often takes a few generations for readers to catch up with them.

You Can Do Anything You Set Your Mind to Doing

And that leads to the final item in the list, the one about maintaining confidence in yourself and your work. This may be the most important part of the entire book. Because I can guarantee that, even if you're not feeling it now, there will come a time when you start to doubt yourself or your talent, or begin to wonder if you're kidding yourself, or dreaming too big, or being unrealistic. The only people who never doubt themselves are people with enormous egos who never try anything new. Some people basically learn how to do one thing, do it their entire lives, and feel pretty darn good about themselves. But that's probably not you. You probably have another job and you're writing in your spare time, wondering if it will ever amount to anything. I understand. This is one reason I host writing conferences and retreats. Yes, the instruction is important, but often even more important is the validation. When people spend an extended period of time surrounded by writers and immersed in learning to write better, it tends to boost their spirits and give them confidence. And every writer needs confidence.

You can be a success. I will even go so far as to say you will be a success. *If you don't quit.* If you don't lose faith. If you keep rolling up your sleeves and doing the work. If you don't lose sight of the fact that this work matters, that writing matters, that your work matters, and you don't lose faith in your ability to do it.

You quite possibly have been confronted with people who do not or did not support your writing aspirations. Parents, siblings, significant others, spouses, etc. "Stop dreaming!" "You're being unrealistic!" "When are you going to put some bread on the table?" "Why don't you just get a nice hobby like stamp collecting?" And so forth. Maybe if you're lucky you also have or had supporters, but the former tend to outnumber the latter. Any time you dream, any time you do something out of the ordinary, you will encounter scoffers. They may be motivated by jealousy or insecurity, but that won't make the words sting any less.

You must ignore them. Put them out of your head. Bury your doubts. Make the leap of faith and keep the pages rolling day after day. Writing is not for the faint-hearted.

As you read the remainder of this book, I hope you will be struck by two thoughts:

1) "Wow. This Bernhardt guy is brilliant. I can totally see how following his process will make my work better."

And…

2) "Wow. That sounds like a lot of work. But I will do it. Because this matters."

Writing sounds like a lot of work because it is. But it will be much easier if you have faith in yourself and your goals. If you remember how important literature and stories have been throughout history, how often books have changed the world. If you tell yourself that any expenditure of time, any amount of work, is justified if it ends with a book that gives you pride and personal satisfaction, and perhaps pleases others as well. Remind yourself why you wanted to write in the first place. Probably you fell in love with books at an early age and wanted to be part of the great conversation we call literature. To achieve anything of that magnitude, you should be willing to put in the time and work necessary.

Editing starts when you first sit down to write—in fact, it starts even earlier. All of writing is a continual process of editing. So as Maria von Trapp recommended, we will "start at the very beginning."

HIGHLIGHTS/EXERCISES

Highlights

1) Writing is a process with no shortcuts that will not jeopardize the quality of your work.

2) Writing is hard.

3) Never give up.

4) Don't wait too long to start.

5) Don't start writing before thinking.

6) Don't stop writing when it's "good enough."

7) Don't allow your writing to be compromised by errors.

8) Don't be afraid to try something new or different.

9) Don't lose confidence in yourself or your work.

10) You can do anything you are determined to do.

Red Sneaker Exercises

1) What are your writing habits? Have you committed to a regular writing procedure? Think about when you are most productive, or when you feel most creative. If you work best in the morning, and your work schedule permits this, make writing the first thing you do each day. (Could you rise earlier each morning?) If not, devise a schedule that guarantees you several hours to write later in the day—on a regular basis. Preferably daily. Read the Writer's Calendar in Appendix A and devise a plan that works for you.

2) Do you have people in your life who do not support your writing goals? Such people can be toxic. Get rid of them. Isolate them as much as possible. If you can't eliminate them entirely, seek companions who will support your dreams. Find a critique group (a supportive one). Even if you don't think their comments improve your work much, you may benefit from contact with other writers. Or take a class at a community college. Or go to a writer's colony or retreat. Stoke your furnace with the fuel you need to succeed.

3) Think about your core idea for your book. Is it genuinely original, or is it basically a rehash of material you've read before or seen on television? If you think it lacks originality, ask yourself: What would make this idea unique? What's something readers haven't seen before? What would be an unexpected twist? What's something they won't see coming? Read the section in *Promising Premise* that discusses Originality and see if you can give your work something to make it stand out. Don't be afraid to try something new or different.

2

PREWRITING

"Most authors would be the first to admit the best of their writing is beyond even them. It comes from someplace outside the conscious realm."

— K.M. WELLAND

The greatest divide in the writing world is not between those who publish and those who don't—it's between those who actually finish a book and those who don't. Those in the first category have a decent chance of publishing; those in the latter category have none—and are far more common. Starting a book is easy, but too many people bog down and quit before they finish.

Why?

I'm sure there are as many reasons as there are writers, but one of the most prominent causes of failure in the writing world is a failure of process. People start writing because they think this is going to be fun, and writing will be a big improvement over their current job, and then...like I said before. Hard work. And they have no process. They start in a blaze of inspiration, and without planning or outlining or fleshing out the story, they write. Pages fly like dust in a whirlwind…until they exhaust the initial idea and have no idea what happens next.

So they stop writing.

Why You Need a Writing Process

You don't want to run around telling people you started a book. You want to tell them you finished a book. Better yet, you want to tell them your book is being published. Which means you need to finish.

Every writer needs a process.

In my book on *Story Structure*, I discussed at greater length some of the institutional, snooty, or romantic ideas that cause people to write without plan or process, so I don't need to repeat them here. But I will say this: There's nothing inherently more artistic about writing without a plan. It just means you're less likely to finish. There's nothing more literary about writing from "inspiration"—which generally means you put down the first idea that pops into your head. Too often that means you're repeating something your subconscious dredged up, not because it's fresh or perfect for your story, but because you've seen it before. Or read it before.

I despair when I hear people at conferences tell me how their characters "came alive and took control of the book." They usually smile with delight because they think this means they're very creative. I do not smile, because I know this means they lack discipline and are unlikely to finish anything publishable. Look, your characters are fictional. They are not real. They do not "come to life." You're just indulging yourself. Maybe some good ideas will come from it, but experience has taught me that it is more likely that this indulgence will derail your book to a point of no return. Writing anything as large and complex as a novel requires application and discipline. Letting your characters run amok may evidence a great imagination, but it may also indicate a lack of work ethic necessary to keep your project on track. Your characters' undirected meanderings will likely be less entertaining to others than they are to you.

In recent years, I've also heard people talking with pride about being "pantsers." The whole pantser movement, that is, people who don't plan but simply write from the seat of their pants, is emblematic of the idea that writing is all fun and games. Pantsers want to do the fun stuff—but they want to skip over hard work like outlining, which is why I have rarely seen a book actually published by anyone who really was a pantser. (Don't be misled by stuff writers say in television interviews, either.) You're goal is not self-entertainment. Your goal is to produce something someone else wants to read.

Writing requires discipline.

The writing process I'm going to recommend basically has four steps (with a lot of sub-steps). A wonderfully creative soul named Betty Flowers wrote some insightful pieces about the writing process. I'm going to borrow her general concepts but modify them so they specifically apply to writing fiction.

Though I am adamant that you need a process, I am not quite arrogant enough to say this is the only possible process. You may experiment as you progress as a writer, finding some sub-steps more valuable than others. That's fine. Do what works for you. But don't skip steps just because they don't sound amusing. Believe me, when you're halfway through a book and for once, you actually know what happens next instead of running out of steam and abandoning the project, you will be glad you worked the process.

As you probably know, your brain is divided into two halves, or hemispheres. MRIs and other neuro-scientific discoveries have allowed us to chart the specific centers of the brain responsible for performing various tasks. Generally speaking, the left hemisphere of the brain is the center of logic, discipline, and critical evaluation. The left brain is tidy, orderly, and wants to keep its ducks in a row. Fortunately, we also have a right hemisphere. The right hemisphere is creative, spontaneous, and instinctive. The right brain wants to try new approaches. Experiment. Get crazy. Throw spaghetti up on the wall and see what sticks. Run stuff up the flagpole and see who salutes. And a host of other clichés that all involve thinking outside the box.

You may believe writing is a right-brain function. But you're wrong. Truth is, writing requires both. Yes, you definitely need creativity and imagination. But you also need discipline and perseverance and the ability to make critical evaluations. Arguably, every draft after the first is about making decisions—what needs to be added and what needs to be removed. That's what revision is.

Writing is not housed in one hemisphere or the other, nor is it a battle between one hemisphere and the other. It's a collaboration, a partnership. Done properly, it can be a winning partnership for you.

BEGIN AT THE BEGINNING

IN THIS BOOK, I WILL DIVIDE THE WRITING PROCESS INTO FOUR phases:

The Inspired Madman
The Intrepid Architect
The Hardworking Hardhat, and

The Court of Last Resort

Let's start with the madman. Seems appropriate for writers, doesn't it? Though please note that I didn't call this stage the Insane Irrational Self-Destructive Madman. Just a madman. A little madness never hurt anyone. If it's channeled creatively.

Let's say you have a strong desire to write, which is the first prerequisite. Let's say that as you drove home from work one afternoon you were suddenly struck with a positively brilliant idea for a book. Something original. With a terrific protagonist (who is not a thinly veiled version of yourself). And a dynamic setting (which is not your hometown). It's time to start writing, yes? Sharpen your pencils. Full steam ahead. Should be done in no time...

Let me suggest an alternate route. First, if you're afraid you'll forget something, write it down. Better safe than sorry. Especially if it came to you in a dream. Dreams have a way of disappearing as soon as we wipe the cobwebs from our eyes. Don't get too romantic for your own good. I've heard a writer say he never writes anything down. "If it's a good idea, I'll remember it when the time comes." Well, bully for him, but I'm not as young as I used to be and sometimes I forget my children's names.

Write down your ideas before you lose them.

Next step: Think about your idea. Yes, this is a stupendously brilliant concept, but we all know you need more than a concept to fill a book. What more can you add? How will the plot develop? What kind of characters do you need? Who's your protagonist? What kind of antagonist do you need to effectively (perhaps sympathetically) oppose the protagonist? What are your three levels of conflict? What would be the most satisfying resolution?

And so forth. Till you have enough to advance to the next level.

I always recommend that at this prewriting stage, you isolate yourself from outside influences and distractions. The best approach is to find a quiet, comfortable place. Close the door. Do not turn on music or any other background distractions. Turn off your cellphone or better yet, leave it in another room. Turn off the pop-ups on your computer screen. Ignore email. And then start thinking about your idea—with a pen in your hand. Write on a piece of paper (you remember paper, right?). Don't edit yourself. Don't censor yourself. Just write whatever pops into your head. True, some of it will be complete garbage that you never use. But if you can improve your book with one good new idea, wasn't it worth the effort? Of course it was.

What you're trying to do here is to tap into your subconscious. Seek inspiration now, when you're forming your plan, rather than later, when you've already committed to a story. Reject the ordinary and the predictable. Delve deeper. See what your subconscious generates. The subconscious does more of your creative work than you probably realize.

By the way, this is also the reason it's important to work on a project consistently, every day till it's done. When you keep your brain tied to a project with that level of consistency, you'll soon find your subconscious is working on it even when your conscious mind is focused on something else. This is why some of your best ideas arrive when you're walking the dog or brushing your teeth—quiet moments when the modern world's many noisemakers are not distracting you. Even when you didn't realize you were thinking about your book—your subconscious was. And it waited for a quiet time to tell you about it.

Use brainstorming and prewriting to build upon your initial ideas.

The late William Zinsler wrote a classic book, *On Writing*. The book focuses on nonfiction, but his words are still relevant: "Your subconscious mind does more writing than you think. Often you'll spend an entire day trying to fight your way through some verbal thicket. Often the solution will come to you the next morning when you shower or drive to work or sit down at your desk. While you slept, your subconscious didn't. A writer is always working."

You may be wondering why I insist that you sit down with a pen and paper. Seems rather primitive, doesn't it? Why did I pay so much for this shiny new laptop if I was going to write with a pen? Here's the thing: sometimes writers need to get away from the electronic screen. When you work with a pen, you tend to think more slowly and more carefully (which is why I will later recommend you do some of your revisions the same way). You are more likely to think freely and creatively when you're performing the physical act of scratching on paper.

Brainstorm with a pen on paper.

Always bear in mind that we are language-based creatures— which is one more reason that we learn and grow so much from reading. Scientists say that language is what defines *Homo sapiens* as a species. We may or may not be the only ones on the planet to have any form of language, but we use it more frequently and more extensively than any other species. Indeed, we are so language-bound that it's difficult for us to conceive of an idea until we put it into words. Have you ever had the experience of trying to make a decision, trying to figure out what to do, but you just can't work it out, so you ask some trusted companion for their opinion. And then, almost magically, as you're explaining the problem—you realize what you need to do. Before your confidante has even spoken. The solution becomes clear as you speak.

Why? Because you put the problem into words. Language. Before, the problem was a nebulous, unclearly defined riddle floating about in your brain. But as soon as you put it into words, you could solve the problem.

So do your brainstorming, your prewriting, with a pen in hand. Okay, just to prove that I'm not inflexible, I will authorize the use of a pencil. Some writing utensil, physically manipulated.

The ideas will flow faster. You may surprise yourself. Sure, you were anxious to get started. You're not going to lose that enthusiasm. Instead, you're going to strengthen it with all the terrific ideas you come up with during this Madman stage of the process —and during the next step as well.

HIGHLIGHTS/EXERCISES

Highlights

1) Every writer needs a process.

2) Writing requires discipline.

3) The writing process has four stages: The Inspired Madman, The Intrepid Architect, The Hardworking Hardhat, and The Court of Last Resort.

4) Write down your ideas before you lose them.

5) Use brainstorming and prewriting to build upon your initial ideas.

6) Brainstorm with a pen on paper.

Red Sneaker Exercises

1) Some writers give themselves quiet time regularly with the

hope of allowing their subconscious to speak to them and generate ideas. Some start the morning on the porch with a cup of coffee. Others spend a little time in the evening in the recliner. Could you carve out a little quiet time for yourself, a time with no noise in the background? If you're strapped for seconds, then finding time to write is probably more important. But having time to think about what you're writing is useful, too. So if possible, devise a time and place that can be your, as Pooh would say, Thoughtful Spot. And go there whenever your schedule permits.

2) Are you a "pantser?" If you are, would you consider humoring me just this once and trying this writing process? Even if you don't much like it, you might find it helps. And if it doesn't, you can go right back to doing what you've always done before. What I'm hoping, of course, is that you'll find this process brings you closer to achieving your writing goals. And maybe the second time you do it, or the third, or the fifteenth—it won't be so difficult.

3) Do you carry a journal? If not, get one. Doesn't have to be large or fancy. But every writer should have a means to jot down ideas so they don't lose them. Yes, I know you can dictate notes into your phone, and if that works for you, fine. But writers are all about language, and the act of physically writing down an idea may actually lead to improving it or expanding upon it. Writing utensils are your friends.

3

THE DREADED OUTLINE

"Whatever joy there is in the writing process can come only when the energies are flowing freely."

— BETTY S. FLOWERS

There is probably no aspect of writing more controversial, or more commonly discussed at writing conferences, than whether writers should outline. You wouldn't think this simple device, often introduced in middle school, would be a source of so much consternation. Or maybe it's *because* of middle school, and being dragged through an unnecessary outline just so you can turn it in, that causes so many aspiring writers to resist the notion. But now that you've reached the Architectural stage of your writing process, the outline is not mere busy work. It's an essential step in the creative construction process. At first, you may perceive it as an annoying obstacle between you and the actual writing, but it's truly a critical step that will not only likely result in a better book, but a better book you get finished sooner than you would have otherwise.

Outlining is essential.

DEPANTSING THE PANTSERS

IT'S TRUE. YOU LISTEN TO WRITERS GABBING ON TELEVISION OR AT conferences, and they almost never talk about outlines. They may in fact deny ever using them. But as Donald Maass and others have observed, author interviews may be fun and entertaining but they are not a reliable source of information about the writing process. Many writers resist talking about outlines because they worry that critics and scholars will deem them less creative. The myth of inspiration, the idea that brilliant ideas arrive by magic in the heads of geniuses, still thrives in many minds, regardless of how inaccurate it may be. If there is any reliable takeaway from books like *Outliers*, it is that genius is not the result of genetics but of applied effort and hard work.

The idea that creating an outline will stifle creativity or prevent your fictional character from being fully realized is completely false. Obviously, when you go beyond the outline and actually write the book, new ideas will occur to you and your story will expand and improve. That does not mean the outline was a waste of time. To the contrary, without the outline, you might never have gotten to those more advanced ideas. You will have more success if you treat writing like work, not entertainment or therapy. That's why I recommended prewriting in the last chapter and why I recommend outlining in this one. Even if it doesn't sound fun.

Writers must be disciplined if they hope to finish something as long and complicated as a novel.

CREATING THE BLUEPRINT

. . .

HAVE YOU ACCEPTED THE FACT THAT YOU MUST OUTLINE, OR AT least that if you do, it will save you time in the long run? Which would you rather do—create a blueprint that includes all the essential elements, or realize five drafts in that you've omitted an essential element, and then try to cram it into a book that's already largely written and doesn't really accommodate the idea? The savvy writer will prefer the former, because the latter is never going to work well.

How do you create a good outline? The first thing you should realize is that no one ever needs to see this but you. Even if you decide to share it with an agent or editor or spouse, you're the only person who's ever going to use it. So it doesn't have to be fancy or exhaustively detailed. You don't have to use Roman numerals. My *Story Structure* book details an outlining procedure that has worked well for many, but it's not the only possible way to do it. I normally just create a numbered list of scenes (not necessarily chapters) that can be easily moved around, added to or subtracted from, as the work proceeds.

Outlining gives you a chance to see the book in its nascent thumbnail state. It makes it easier to view the big picture, to remind yourself where this is going. Can you see the three-act structure—the beginning, middle, and end? Can you identify the inciting incident? Have you made it big enough to turn your protagonist's world upside-down? Can you see how that sets your protagonist on a journey or quest? Can you see how the obstacles your protagonist will face escalate as the book proceeds? To quote James William Johnson, "A working outline, made to serve as a guide for a future composition, can prevent the sort of obvious muddles...that often occur when we do not think something out before we formally deliver it...as a piece of writing."

In *Perfecting Plot*, I discussed the importance of creating increasingly difficult challenges for the protagonist to face on his or her journey toward the climax. An outline may show you that the biggest scene is in the middle, not the end, or that no new complications are introduced for too long a time. I also discussed the three levels of conflict—internal, external, and personal. Are all three present in your character's journey? If you see that one is missing, here's a great chance to introduce a subplot that will enrich the story, before you've already written so much of the book that inserting a new thread becomes awkward or frustrating or impossible. Do you need a romantic interest, a parental conflict, an interloping supervisor? Then put it in. Are you missing an internal conflict? Few books will succeed if the protagonist is not dealing with something psychologically or emotionally in addition to confronting the external problem.

Sometimes early writers make the mistake of having their outline focus exclusively on the plot. Don't forget about character and characterization when you're outlining. In *Creating Character*, I discussed how characterization can be used to provide essential information about your character's internal makeup without overtly stating it—that is, showing rather than telling. Plant some of those details in the outline to ensure they come out in the book in a natural, rather than a forced, manner. Details like the kind of car your character drives or what they order in a restaurant may end up inspiring or enlivening entire scenes.

The main characters, certainly the protagonist, need to be on a character arc, which generally means a dialectical journey from one place to its opposite—from innocence to wisdom, from insecurity to confidence, from sin to redemption. That should be added to your outline just as surely as the plot. In many ways, it is your plot, or at least an essential element of it. Make sure you plant the stepping stones throughout the book. The steps should be gradual. Any overnight character changes will seem forced. But there should be a point somewhere in the middle where the reader sees the change beginning to occur, and of course, a place at the end where the journey is complete.

The only essential element of your book that I don't think necessarily needs to be in the outline is Theme. If you've already got your theme, you know what you want it to be and want to make sure it comes out, then by all means put it down on paper. But in many cases I do think theme develops organically during the writing process. I would even be willing to say that a theme unnaturally imposed on a book often seems clunky and contrived and less successful. So I'm content to let you save that for a later point in the process.

Outlining starts after you've given this book a lot of thought.

Another reason people struggle with outlines is that they try to write them before they've given the book any serious thought. Maybe they have the general premise, but nothing more. You need to do the prewriting discussed in the previous chapter. I typically get the core idea for my next book while I'm still writing the previous one. Truth is, I usually get several good ideas for the next book before I've finished the last one—and that's good.

Now pay attention to this: Do not stop writing the book you're on just because you're so fond of some new idea you got. Abandoned books are rarely finished. Force yourself to finish the present one, whether you think it's going well or not, before you move to the next. Otherwise, all the time you spent on that book will be wasted.

By the time I'm ready to write the next book, I usually find that one of my many ideas has risen to the surface, has caught hold of my imagination in a more powerful way. That's the one I write. Or better yet, I've concocted some way to combine all my ideas into one magnificent book, which of course increases the chance that it will be rippling with developments and complications on every page.

If you've put sufficient pre-thinking into your book, writing the outline should not be that much of a problem. Look through all those ideas you put down. Keep the good ones and arrange them in some logical order. Probably the beginning and the end will come easily, and you'll struggle with the middle. That's fine. Endure the struggle. First time you do it, it may consume several days of hard work. After a little practice, I predict you'll find yourself kicking out outlines in a day or two. Keep the outline open on your desktop so you can refer to it often. Or print it and place it on your desk so you can scribble ideas and notes when appropriate.

One last thing to say about your outline. This is a road map, not a cage. New ideas will come to you as you actually write the book. That's good. Add them to your outline. Keep plussing it. Your outline is still there to make sure you don't waste time staring out the window wondering what happens next. When you're lost in the minutiae of a particular chapter, it's easy to lose track of the larger journey. Where is this book going? What's the endgame? No worries. Just glance at your outline and you're right back on track. Your outline is the candle that never blows out, the light that keeps shining to make sure you don't crash on the craggy shore.

Recently, I wrote a book (my 46th) with such a strong idea of where it was going and what would happen next I just decided, despite all my years of experience, to plunge in without an outline. What happened? What always happens. I got about ten chapters in and crapped out. It's always that middle section, isn't it? Fortunately, I didn't have to scrap everything I'd done. I just did what I should have done in the first place. I wrote my outline. Then I finished the book. I did have to rework what I had already written quite a bit. But the outline got me back where I needed to be.

HIGHLIGHTS/EXERCISES

Highlights

1) Outlining is essential.

2) Writers must be disciplined if they ever hope to finish something as long and complicated as a novel.

3) Outlining starts after you've given this book a lot of thought.

Red Sneaker Exercises

1) This time the exercise is obvious: start your outline. You may find it easiest to do the first fifteen scenes or so first, because you probably have a good idea who your main characters are and how the story kicks off. Then you may prefer to go to the ending, because you probably already have some thoughts on that, too. Eventually you have to go to the middle, but that will be easier once you have the rest on paper. Can you connect the dots? How do your characters get from the first fifteen scenes to the last fifteen scenes?

2) You may choose to show your outline to others to get their input, and if they are experienced partners, that's fine. But don't worry about the fact that the outline may not seem particularly interesting in and of itself. It's not meant to be read. It's a resource. Without dialogue, the characters won't come alive on the page, and without blow-by-blow detail, the action scenes won't come alive and the big surprises won't seem particularly gasp-inducing. Fear not. When did you ever use a road map and think it was a terrific read? Just make sure you have the essential elements to make a fabulous book.

3) Save your outline somewhere safe, somewhere other than (or in addition to) the computer on which you plan to write the book. Email it to yourself, if nothing else, and don't delete the email. You put a lot of work into this and you don't want to lose it.

4

THE FIRST CUT IS THE DEEPEST

"Writing is easy. You just open a vein and bleed."

— RED SMITH

In case you're wondering, the chapter heading is really just another way of saying, The first draft is the hardest. Or so it seems to me. I have heard other writers say differently, but I notice those tend to be pantsers, so conclude what you will. As you transition from Architect to Hardhat, you may find the task gets trickier and takes forever. Don't worry about it. You're tough and you're in this for the long haul.

No matter how good you are, the first draft will take time. Probably months. Possibly years. In the film *Limitless*, Bradley Cooper wrote a book in about four days, but that doesn't happen in real life. It will be a time-consuming process, but it's the only way to finish a book. The first draft may be the most important draft, but it is the most time-consuming. This is where you prove that you have the right stuff, that you have what it takes to get the job done.

The first draft is the most important thing you will ever write.

Building Blocks

The first draft is when you move out of the more creative right-brain territory into the more structured left brain. You're not leaving right-brain land altogether. If you don't bring any creativity to this first draft, it's not going to be terribly interesting. But if you don't have any structure or organization, it's going to be a huge mess, and you don't want that either. You want something you can build on in subsequent drafts, something that makes your later work easier, not harder. The Hardhat builder must create the best structure possible or the building will fall apart later.

I think of the first draft as a big brain dump. Basically, you're trying to get all those ideas and all that information you have in your head down on paper—in a somewhat organized form that actually tells a story in detail. It's difficult if not impossible to do much refining while the ideas are still floating around in immaterial form in your brain. Once you have them on paper (or the electronic simulacrum of paper), refinement is easier.

The first draft is a brain dump. Get all the ideas floating around in your head down on paper.

It's important that you don't try to revise while writing the first draft. The time for revision will come later. Right now, you want to keep the flow flowing. Don't lose your momentum. I've heard one writer compare premature revision to applying the clutch while you're still driving up the hill. Don't throw out your clutch! Keep the pages flowing! George Miller wrote, "Polishing at an early stage is usually a complete waste of time." So don't worry about whether your first draft is pretty or not. I've been doing this for a while, but nonetheless, every time I write a first draft I think, When did I forget how to write? This is terrible!

Then I go back and read it and find it's not quite as bad as I thought. But it does need work. So I do the work.

PREMATURE EMASCULATION

THE TRUTH IS, REGARDLESS OF HOW MUCH THOUGHT YOU'VE PUT into your project, no matter how smart you are or how much research you've done, you never really know what you have till you've completed and read your first draft. After that, you can read the whole thing and understand what you've got and not got, what works and what doesn't, what are the strengths and weaknesses. That brilliant denouement that only occurred to you as you wrote it may have changed the tone or focus of the entire project. Perhaps you stumbled across your theme as you wrote and realized that required a scene to be added or subtracted, a character to be added or given a gender change, a motivation to be altered. Only after you've finished the first draft can you see the big picture.

To put it more succinctly, I hope you didn't spend a week revising and perfecting chapter three, only to realize that chapter three has to go.

You've probably heard people say that writers must "kill their darlings." What this usually means is that if you've composed a turn of phrase that's particularly clever or lovely, it probably calls attention to itself. And if it calls attention to itself, you need to cut it, because readers should be immersed in the story, not thinking about how clever the writer is. Similarly, if you get to the end of the first draft and realize the tone or direction or focus of the book has altered, you will have to do some cutting and revision, perhaps more than you anticipated. That's fine—do the work that needs to be done. But I don't want you to waste a lot of time during the first draft beautifying language that will end up on the cutting room floor. So save the revising for later.

Don't revise during the first draft. Start revising after you've completed the first draft.

WRITE THE LONG GAME

ANOTHER OF THE MANY REASONS TO OUTLINE IS SO YOU CAN JUDGE how many scenes you need to complete your book. If you've read what's on the shelves in your field or genre, you probably have an idea what the approximate length of your book should be. Compose your outline accordingly. If you have any writing experience, you should know how long your scenes tend to run. If you have no idea, assume an average scene length of about five pages. After all, you want a speedy pace that will keep readers glued to the page. No one is likely to get bored with a five-page scene.

So how many scenes does that mean you need to complete the book? Do the math, then write your outline to that length.

Or perhaps, ten to twenty percent longer. Here's the thing. When you start revising the book—after the first draft is complete—you will almost certainly make cuts. You may add a few scenes too, but if you're maintaining a quick pace and observing the hallmarks of professional writing discussed in my book *Sizzling Style*, you're probably making more cuts than additions. What if you realize the book would be improved if you made cuts but you're hesitant to do it because it will make the overall book too short?

Don't let that happen. Write the first draft long. Mind you, don't pad it. Don't insert the unnecessary. But if you know your draft is longer than it actually needs to be, then you won't cry too many salty tears when you have to perform some minor surgery. In the world of fiction, tighter is almost always better.

Make your first draft longer than it needs to be.

By the way, when you must make serious cuts to your manuscript—never throw anything away. Word processors make it simple to maintain a file of cut scenes. Odds are, you will never use them. But no one knows what the future holds. It is just possible that somewhere down the line you'll be preparing to write a scene for another book and realize—I have just the thing! And it's already written! Steve Berry told me a story about cutting a major action sequence from one of his early manuscripts simply because the book was too long. But several books later, he needed an action scene, and the scene he cut earlier fit the bill perfectly. He had to change the location but little else. I can't guarantee that will happen to you (it has never happened to me). But it doesn't hurt to save your work, just in case.

Save everything.

The Writer's Calendar (Appendix A) is a week-by-week guide to finishing your first draft in about six months. Again, this is meant to be an advisory guide, not a forced march. Adapt it to your own writing procedures and your own schedule. You may have more or less time to write each day, and obviously that will impact how long it takes to get the job done. All that matters is that you finish the book.

Some people use support groups, critique groups, writing coaches, contests, NaNoWrMo, or other such devices to keep them writing. Fundamentally, every writer must possess drive and desire. If you have drive and desire, you'll get the job done, regardless of how long it takes. But if these external motivators work for you, use them. Just don't get caught in the trap of spending more time thinking about writing or talking about writing than you actually spend writing. Don't talk about your book so much you're sick of it before you've finished that first draft. And by all means don't start writing just to please or amuse your writing group. You goal is to be published, right? That will require a manuscript that appeals to far more than a handful of close friends.

I do think everyone benefits from some form of support, regardless of whether you share your early drafts. The old cliché is that writing is the loneliest business. True, when you're working and it's just you and your word processor, you're in isolation. (Sort of—as I write this, I'm sitting on the sofa and my wife and daughters are having an animated conversation in the kitchen. I've learned to focus.) But everyone needs to get out and interact with humans on occasion. Everyone needs someone who supports this wacky dream of publishing a book. Find that person and cherish them. Find your tribe.

No one is alone. Not even writers.

The quote I put at the top of this chapter is possibly the most famous quote in the world of writing, but I think it is also the most frequently misunderstood. Yes, Smith made the point that writing is tough, just as I have. He was a sportswriter who wrote a regular column, and this quote came in response to critics (everyone has them) who suggested that writing a column was easy and "wasn't really writing." His response dramatically makes the point that writing is as hard as any job ever was, and I would agree. But as Paul Gallico wrote in reply, "It is only when you open your veins and bleed onto the page a little that you connect with your reader."

Gallico was dead right, so let that be your solace on those days when the words don't come as easily as you wish and it seems as though you've been working on this first draft since the dawn of time. You're doing this for a reason. And the more blood you spill, the more likely your words will make a positive difference in someone's life.

HIGHLIGHTS/EXERCISES

Highlights

1) The first draft is the most important thing you will ever write.

2) The first draft is a brain dump. Get all the ideas floating around in your head on paper.

3) Don't revise during the first draft. Start revising after you've completed the first draft.

4) Make your first draft longer than it needs to be.

5) Save everything.

6) No one is alone. Not even writers.

Red Sneaker Exercises

1) One of the important preparatory items covered in the Writer's Calendar (Appendix A) is creating a place where you can

work. You may not have the luxury of renting office space or buying a fancy desk. None of that matters much. You should have a comfortable chair, because you don't want to develop back problems before the book is done (or after). Create that comfortable space and commit to being there on a regular basis, whether you feel like it or not. If you only write when you're "in the mood," you will never finish anything.

2) You also need quiet. If like me you've raised children, you may get to the point where you can write anywhere, but that's a talent you develop with experience. You probably won't have as much time as you'd like to write either, so get the people around you to respect your writing time and basically leave you alone. (The occasional quiet delivery of coffee or ice cream may be acceptable.)

3) When you finally finish that first draft, celebrate. You've earned it. Go out to eat. Throw yourself a little party. (You'll probably spend half the time remembering everything you left out of the book and making notes on what to add later.) You could even take a day off. One. And then start the second draft.

5

WRITING IS REWRITING

"I have rewritten—often several times—every word I have ever published."

— VLADIMIR NABOKOV

James Michener, a writer I've enjoyed since the sixth grade, said, "I'm not a very good writer. But I'm a great rewriter." I personally doubt the first part. But I absolutely believe the latter. Revision is when the magic happens. Even if you're convinced your first draft was complete garbage, it doesn't matter, because pixie dust will be in the air as you revise. Revision is of such importance that I've heard major writers say, "Writing *is* Rewriting." They aren't suggesting that rewriting is all there is. They're suggesting that it's the part that matters most. It's what separates mediocre writers from great writers.

Writing is rewriting.

And you all want to be great writers, correct? So now it's time to call to order The Court of Last Resort. Here comes the Judge. From this point forward, it's almost entirely left-brain work. The judge must scrutinize what's on the page, objectively and cold-bloodedly, and make a determination about what goes and what stays. Sometimes you have to be ruthless. Sometimes you might even break your heart (a little). But to whatever extent is possible, the judge has to keep sentiment and emotion out of the decision-making process. Judgments must be made based upon a cool-headed determination about how to make the book as good as it can possibly be. This process should elate you, because you know you're making your work better. But if at any point it starts to get you down, please remember the immortal words of J. Russell Lynes: "No one dislikes to be edited as much as he dislikes not to be published."

Revision is Essential

OF COURSE YOU REVISE. THIS IS OBVIOUS. AT LEAST, I HOPE IT'S obvious. Who would ever think you would get a book of any quality in one draft? And yet, for a variety of reasons, this eludes many writers, even those I know are absolutely smart people (in other areas). Fleshing out a great idea can and should be an exciting process, even though it takes forever and a day. If you put a climax and denouement on it that pleases you, it's only natural that you would be excited about what you've got. Don't let that excitement fool you into thinking you don't need to do any more work. You do.

In addition to writing for several decades now, I've also run several publishing houses. I know for a fact that some of the over-the-transom manuscripts we received were first drafts. Believe it or not, some people actually admitted it in their cover letters. "This is my first draft, but I'd be willing to do some editing if you think it needs it." No, I am not making this up.

Two things I can tell you with certainty. One: Yes, your first draft needs editing, if not a complete overhaul. Two: No publishing house editor in the world today has time to do it for you. The people we call "editors," at least in the larger houses, spend their workdays in meetings and conferences, not redlining manuscripts. Your book must be largely ready to go or no one will bother with it. Probably no literary agent will either. They simply don't have time, and why would they want to anyway, when there are so many great manuscripts floating around? They could much more easily choose something that doesn't need major work.

I have also encountered beginning writers who have a vague notion that their book needs work, but decide to hire outside editors to do it for them, or worse, "book doctors." Here are my thoughts. First, avoid all people who call themselves book doctors. Second, if you want an editor, hire someone with a track record that shows they know what publishable manuscripts are because they've actually written some. I've had people arrive at my writing retreats after spending over five thousands dollars on editors they found in magazine ads who gave them some of the worst advice I've heard in my life.

You need to learn how to edit your books yourself. And the only way you will learn to do that is by doing it.

Mind you, after you've extensively revised and worked the book to the point that you think there's nothing more you know to do to it, it might be smart to obtain outside opinions. We'll discuss that later. Be don't go there prematurely. The all-important early revisions need to be performed by you, because no one knows your story, your intentions, and your goals better.

Here's something else to bear in mind. Only amateurs think every word they've written is written in indelible ink. The people at conferences who insist that their book is perfect are the ones who don't get published. Their inability to receive criticism prevents them from growing.

Even *To Kill a Mockingbird* went through several drafts after an editor got it—and each draft made the book better. If Harper Lee had refused to listen, had refused to revise, we wouldn't have the classic we have today. Here's the truth: Amateurs fall in love with every word they write. Professionals destroy 95% of all the words they write—because they know they can do better. So they cut, add, revise, rearrange, or whatever the book needs. That's how you get to a publishable novel. I think Colette said it best: "Put down everything that comes into your head and then you're a writer. But an author is one who can judge his own stuff's worth, without pity, and destroy most of it."

Learn to edit yourself. And be willing to do it.

THE ALL-IMPORTANT SECOND DRAFT

OKAY, SO YOU'VE FINISHED THE FIRST DRAFT, TAKEN A DAY OFF, AND now you're ready to get back to work. Where do you start?

At the beginning. Read the manuscript from top to bottom. As much as possible, pretend that you are not the writer but a causal reader who picked up the book having no idea where the story was headed or what would happen next. Read it all in a sitting or two if possible.

Did you enjoy it? Did you find it satisfying? Or, more likely, if you're truly being objective, did you find it has some problems?

That's going to be the focus of your second draft, and probably one or two thereafter. Fixing the problems.

You may begin by performing some major surgery. (I guess now you're the book doctor.) You may realize that some scenes need to be added. Maybe a relationship isn't sufficiently developed to create the emotional reaction you want in the denouement. Maybe the climax ends too quickly, or the protagonist prevails too easily. If so, it's time for a transplant. Add some new scenes.

You may realize you've written some scenes that don't need to be in the book. If they don't advance the narrative, and they don't contribute anything else, eliminate them. Excise the diseased cells and the body will be stronger. Anything that slows down the pace, that duplicates material found elsewhere, needs to go. Kurt Vonnegut said that he revised his manuscripts word-by-word, interrogating each word, asking "Does this word have to be in here?" Not *could* it be there, mind you, but *must* it be there. If the answer was no, the word was gone. The happy result was terse, taut, finely crafted novels that are still a pleasure to read.

Every writer has their own particular style bugaboos. I tend to overuse dashes as a devise for speeding up the pace of dialogue. Some people overuse helping verbs (was, were, am, etc.). Some people can't shake degree adverbs (very, really, pretty, clearly, etc.). Some tend to use the same words repetitively. Generally speaking, you never want a word to repeat in a sentence, and the more attention-catching ones shouldn't repeat in the same paragraph. Maybe not even on the same page. Whatever it is you know you tend to do, these early drafts are a good time to fix it. I told you not to edit yourself as you wrote the first draft, but now you should. Use that Find and Replace function to scour your entire manuscript, removing the offending words and replacing them with exciting, vibrant words.

I've included a "Search and Destroy" list in one of the appendices that you may use as a guide for this stage of the editing process. I've also included a summary of some of my most important style tips, the ones that most commonly plague the manuscripts I've seen at my writing retreats. Run through that list and make sure your book is written professionally. Don't give agents and editors an easy excuse to dismiss your manuscript. Make the writing just as sharp as it needs to be.

THE THIRD DRAFT, FOURTH, FIFTH...

. . .

IN MOST CASES, ESPECIALLY WITH BEGINNING WRITERS, THERE WILL be other problems that need to be addressed at an early stage. I hope you will be honest and objective and fix what needs to be fixed. Ask yourself these questions:

1. Do the major characters come alive on the page?
2. Does the plot move forward at a steady, engaging pace, never slowing, and quickening toward the end?
3. Is the climax a satisfying resolution to the book?
4. Does the last page leave the reader with a satisfying emotional resonance?

NOTHING CAN BE MORE CHALLENGING THAN BEING HARD ON yourself, but it's the only way to make sure you've written a first-rate book. Good writing takes time. One of the biggest problems in the writing world today is that, with the game-changing advent of eBooks and online purchasing, publishers have started encouraging their most popular writers to turn out multiple books a year. The inevitable result is that writers can't spend as much time on each book as they once did, and the quality of their work declines as a result. (Then sales decline and eventually the publisher fires them, blaming the author, and replacing them with someone they haven't milked dry yet.) If I could, I would make each reader of this book raise their right hand and swear they will never release a book before they've spent as much time as they need to make it the best book it can possibly be. But since I can't, I will advise you to answer each of the questions above and revise accordingly.

When I revise, I spend one entire pass through the manuscript focusing on character. With crime fiction, mysteries, thrillers, and such, the plot is typically so intricate and important that it's easy to let the characters become ciphers, stick figures running and jumping through the motions. This is the death knell to writing success, particularly if you hope to be writing for a while. The only reason anyone buys a book in a series is because they like the series character. And no matter how many times you've thrilled and delighted your readers, the first time you give them a book that disappoints, there's a good chance they'll drop you from their buying list.

As discussed in *Creating Character*, not all of the dozens of characters in your novel can or should be fully developed. But the main ones, typically the most important four or five, should be unique and interesting, not thinly veiled duplicates of characters found in abundance in television and cinema. You need to make them come alive on the page, to make the reader want to read more about them. So I spend a draft focusing on those all-important characters, making sure they're doing their job. Remember that your characters shouldn't all sound alike. If every character's dialogue speaks with the same voice (probably yours), you're not allowing your characters to distinguish themselves properly.

I also spend a pass-through making sure the plot holds together. That means every time a character talks about what they've done, provides an alibi, or explains what happened in the past, I know whether their explanation is true (and if it isn't, why they're lying). It means every time some jaw-dropping, gasp-inducing, chapter-ending event occurs, I understand who committed this horrifying deed and why (even if the reader won't find out until much later). Basically, I make sure the story adds up. I know there are lots of stories out there about writers who didn't—Raymond Chandler admitting he had no idea who killed the chauffeur in *The Big Sleep*, etc.—but that's probably not going to fly in today's publishing world. First time someone posts a one-star review on your Amazon page complaining that your story doesn't hold together, you're going to wish you'd spent more time on the plot.

Pacing is of critical importance. Robin Cook used to say that as he read novels, he would take his pulse (he's a physician) to see if the book excited him. If it did, he tried to figure out why. You can probably tell if a book is exciting you without taking your pulse. So if you're reading your manuscript and the story seems to lag, you need to figure out why. Is there too much talking and not enough action? Is the action simply a blow-by-blow description with no emotional involvement (often a problem for sex scenes, too)? Perhaps it can be fixed with incisive editing, such as varying your sentence length or breaking up long paragraphs. Long paragraphs will always slow down the pace of a book and, even worse, tempt readers to skip them. And if they start skipping, soon they'll be skimming…and from there it's a short walk to putting the book down. Don't give your reader any place where they can cheerfully put down your book.

The climax is probably the most important group of scenes in your book. Readers have waited for it a long time, so you must give them the big deal they want. A quick resolution of a problem the protagonist has wrestled with for three hundred pages will not satisfy. You want to read and reread your climax, making sure it ties up all the dangling threads and gives readers the satisfaction they want. You're not spending too much time on the climax so long as every time you reread it, you find a way to make it better.

To be fair, there are some books out there, particularly in the world of popular fiction, that don't seem to conclude with any sort of emotional resonance, and they still survive. Perhaps some readers are satisfied with a book that simply entertains for a few hours. But I think the best books, the ones people remember long after they've finished reading them, give something more than just a plot payoff. They give an emotional payoff as well. They provide a moment of sweetness, or a fresh idea, or an unexpected yet insightful twist. Can you put something like that on your last page or pages? If you can, you may find you've written a story with far more staying power.

I don't know how long all this revision will take you. Theoretically, each draft should take a little less time, because each pass there's less to change. And all of these drafts combined probably won't take as long as it took to write your first draft. But it will take time. Don't worry about that. Don't get in a hurry. Keep your eyes on the prize. Never forget how tough the publishing market is. If you're going to break in, you're going to have to give this work everything you've got. Your plan is to produce a book so fantastic that agents and editors will kneel before you and take your book where you want it to go. So it's worth the investment.

By the time you've completed drafts focusing on your personal bugaboos, character, pacing, plot, etc., you're probably at the end of your fifth draft. At least. Good for you. It may be time for a break. But just to be sure, go through all the questions in the Fifth Draft Checklist in the Appendices. If you can answer all those questions in a way that satisfies you, fantastic. You've earned a break. You can take a week off now before you proceed. In fact, it's a good idea to do so, because I don't want you to get to the point where you're so sick of reading this you can't work on it any more. That would be disastrous—because you're not done yet.

Ask yourself the difficult, more detailed questions in the Checklist. All of these questions are based on the problems I've seen most frequently in well-honed novels I've either edited or seen at retreats. Is there any reason to like your characters, or to care about them? That's essential to sustaining reader interest (even bad guys can be liked, in a perverse way). Does the protagonist's motivation deepen as the story develops? Do the obstacles become more daunting? Do the stakes increase? Is the story predictable? Does this story say what you want it to say? These questions may direct your attention to work that still needs to be done. If so, don't hesitate to do it. At this point, we're talking about minor surgery. But those minor touches need to be made. Every question on the checklist is there for a reason—to make sure your manuscript has the essential elements that have made books successful since the dawn of storytelling.

Don't sell yourself short now. Keep revising as long as you can make it better.

And when you're finished with that? All done?

You wish. Now it's time to proofread. Did you think you'd already done that? Wrong.

HIGHLIGHTS/EXERCISES

Highlights

1) Writing is rewriting.

2) Learn to edit yourself. And be willing to do it.

3) Do each of the major characters come alive on the page?

4) Does the plot move forward at a steady, engaging pace, never slowing, and quickening toward the end?

5) Is the climax a satisfying resolution to the book?

6) Does the last page leave the reader with a satisfying emotional resonance?

7) Don't sell yourself short now. Keep revising as long as you can make it better.

Red Sneaker Exercises

1) Look at the Search and Destroy list in Appendix B. I've compiled this based upon reading hundreds of manuscripts. You probably already instinctively avoid using or overusing some of them…but no draft is perfect. Go down the list, putting each word into Find (under the Edit tab in Microsoft Word). If you're searching a book-length document, and the result is a one-digit number, then you're probably okay. If you see a larger number, try to reduce it. Find more powerful ways of expressing yourself.

2) Review the list of Style Tips attached as Appendix C. (Most of these are discussed in greater detail in my book *Sizzling Style*.) Again, let Find and Replace be your friend. Review the list before each pass through your manuscript. That may seem repetitive, but the more you review the list, the more this process will become second nature to you. In time, you will probably find you have a tendency to commit some style errors, such as excessive reliance on helping verbs, or too many sentences starting with indefinite pronouns like "It" and "There." The more you practice excising these flaws, the less frequently they'll appear in your work in the future. Even without consciously editing yourself, you'll find yourself doing it less. And the ones you miss the first time through, you will definitely catch during the second.

3) After you've taken several passes through your manuscript and you think that you've eliminated the major flaws, take a look at the Fifth Draft Checklist. These questions are deeper, more profound, and will probably require more thought, more honesty, and more introspection. You may even be tempted to ask for outside opinions, though I personally think the time to show the work to others is after you've done everything you can think of to do to it yourself. Don't let the amount of work left to do get your down. Your goal is an important one—making sure your book accomplishes everything you want it to accomplish. Whether the questions lead you to minor changes or major ones,

take the time to work through the list. I've seen students try to fix significant character or motivation problems by adding a sentence here or there. That's probably not going to cut it. These problems can't be resolved with a quick fix. Do the work that needs to be done to produce the book you want your name on.

6

CATCHING THE GLITCHES

"Writing and rewriting are a constant search for what it is one is saying."

— JOHN UPDIKE

L et me start this chapter by making a distinction between revision and proofreading. Revision, the subject of the previous chapter, is making substantive changes to ensure your book achieves its goals. Proofreading, the subject of this chapter, is about eliminating niggling errors that, although seemingly trivial, still matter. And both revision and proofreading combined are how you achieve what Updike described in the quote above—expressing what you want to say. If you have something to communicate and you want others to hear it, then you must say it well and powerfully, not halfheartedly with half-baked, flawed writing.

PROOFREADING MATTERS

. . .

LIKE IT OR NOT, SOME READERS ARE GRAMMAR FIENDS OR nitpickers at heart. Perhaps even some of you. How many of you have read a book and then made a little tsking noise as you encountered a typo? Perhaps even sent an angry email to the author berating her or her publisher for inexcusable sloppiness. Why? Why do people get so upset about such small matters? I'm not sure, but I know it happens. Note how many angry Amazon reviews revolve around the critic's detection of a typo or two. Some of it may be the desire to flaunt linguistic superiority by bragging that they caught something others missed. In many cases, though, people are inarticulately expressing their disappointment with the story, even though they're zeroing in on the typos.

Part of writing a good story is establishing the suspension of disbelief. You want the reader to become so immersed in the story that they forget they're reading a book. You want them to inhabit your fictional world. You want the real world to disappear while the reader is absorbed in something magical you've created. And coming across a typo, however minor, shatters the illusion. It draws the reader out of the story and causes them to start thinking about the writer (not in a positive way). You may get them back. But then again, you may not.

The same problem exists in every other professional realm. In the business world, as soon as you turn in a document containing typos, you've eroded your reader's confidence in you and your work. You invite your boss (or judge) to think, "Well, if I can't trust him on the small stuff, why should I trust him on anything important?" It's no different in fiction. Keep your reader focused on your brilliant story, not your human fallibility.

Sadly, these kinds of errors have become more common in the eBook era, in part because publishers are rushing books to print and in part because authors are publishing their own books without adequate editorial oversight. I have no problem with self-publishing. I'm in favor of anything that puts more power where it should be, in the hands of creators rather than corporations. But if you self-publish sloppy work, it will cost you, and you will have no one to blame but yourself.

Do you remember the famous words spoken by Neil Armstrong when he set foot on the moon back in 1969? Chances are you have a glimmer of an idea what he said, even if you weren't alive at the time, but you may not know the exact words. Don't feel bad. Truth is, no one is sure of the exact words. But it's one or the other of the following two sentences:

THAT'S ONE SMALL STEP FOR A MAN, ONE GIANT LEAP FOR mankind.

Or...

That's one small step for man, one giant leap for mankind.

WHY THE DISCREPANCY? IF YOU LISTEN TO THE RECORDING OF THIS historic moment, it sounds like he said the second version. Granted, he was a long way off, radio communication was far from perfect, and there's a lot of static. But it still sounds like the second. In fact, professional sound engineers have skillfully removed all the static...and it still sounds like the second.

But Armstrong maintained that he said the first version. At any rate, that's what he meant to say. This line had been worked out in advance, someone probably realizing that this historic moment could be enhanced with some stirring words. Armstrong practiced the line and knew it by heart.

I don't think this sort of drama came naturally to him. On the Internet now you can hear the entire moon landing broadcast, the five minutes before the famous line and the five minutes after. Everything else he says is scientific observation, clinical, precise. And then, just as he steps off the ladder, he delivers the famous line.

Or thought he did.

It's just possible that as he was about to become the first person to set foot on a heavenly body other than Earth, he may have had more pressing concerns on his mind. But he appears to have muffed the line.

Why are people still talking about this all these years later? After all, the only difference is the inclusion or exclusion of "a," a tiny little article adjective, the smallest non-capitalized word in the English language. Who cares? What difference does it make?

Quite a bit, as it turns out. The first version, the pre-scripted version with the "a," makes sense. This is a small step for Armstrong, the guy stepping off the ladder onto the moon, but it's a huge technological leap forward for all of mankind.

But the other version, without the "a," sounds as if he's using "man" in the same sense as "mankind," that is, to refer to *Homo sapiens* as a whole. In which case the statement is contradictory. He first says it's a small step for mankind, then says it's a big one. This makes no sense.

So at a crucial historical moment, overheard by about three billion people, the meaning was muddled if not lost, all because a single letter was omitted.

Are you starting to see why it's important to proofread your work?

This is not the only time in history or literature that a little word made a big difference. Shelley's notes show that he spent an enormous amount of time going back and forth on the question of whether his famous ode should be titled "To *a* Skylark" or "To *the* Skylark" (as it was). Was he writing about a particular skylark or skylarks in general? It makes a difference.

Would you read a book titled *A Godfather* or *A Great Gatsby* or *A Wizard of Oz*? Of course not. The definite article makes it sound much more important.

One more sad truth—there has never been a perfect book and there never will be. Even with books that have been professionally edited and proofed by many hands, usually one or two typos slip through the cracks. Happily now, in the digital age, they can be fixed relatively easily. Perfection may not be obtainable, at least not at first. But if you work hard, you can keep errors to a minimum that will not imperil your success as a writer.

STRIVING FOR PERFEKTION

YES, THAT TYPO WAS INTENTIONAL. BECAUSE THERE'S NO SUCH thing as perfection, especially in writing. Or any other art form.

Before we discuss how to eliminate minor typos, misspellings, incorrect verb tense, etc., let's consider how these errors occur. Why do mistakes crop up in manuscripts that have been read many times by smart, well-educated people?

Sometimes our brains fool us. When the brain knows what the sentence is supposed to say, or can tell where this sentence is going, it inserts words that are not actually on the page. Have you ever inadvertently left out an "a" or a "the?" It's easy to do, because even if it isn't there, your brain will put it in for you. The same is true for misspellings and other errors that creep into manuscripts but are easily overlooked. In effect, your brain becomes a cranial AutoCorrect (and you know how perfect that is). So to effectively proofread, we need to "unfool" the brain. We need to prevent it from being so damn helpful.

The four most common proofreading techniques are:

1. **Reading the manuscript backwards.**
2. **Reading the pages or sentences out of order.**
3. **Reading the manuscript aloud.**
4. **Getting someone else to do it.**

Not necessarily in that order.

Did your jaw drop a little when I mentioned reading the book backwards?

Believe it or not, there are writers who actually do this. The idea is that because you're reading the story backwards, your brain stops anticipating what's coming next. Unless you are so brilliant your brain thinks both forward and backward, it won't be able to anticipate what should be in the next sentence. Consequently you will notice if you've omitted an article adjective or used the wrong form of "its." This is definitely the "hair shirt" approach to editing. It's slow work, but I'm told, amazingly effective.

You may have noticed that I'm using phrases like "I'm told" and "I've heard." That's because I've never done this and I never will. Life is too short. It sounds painful. Surely there is another approach.

For me, option two is more merciful. Print it, throw the pages up in the air, reassemble them in random order, and read through them that way. Since the story is not being read sequentially, it won't make any coherent sense, so your brain might be less inclined to insert words that aren't actually there. But you're still reading left to right, as we do in the English language, and the sentences still make sense, which is essential for catching other errors, such as subject-verb agreement and whether you should use "who" or "whom."

As I mentioned earlier, at some point in your proofreading, you should push away from the word processor, print the manuscript, and edit with a pen. Did you get the shakes when I said "push away from the word processor?" I'm not dissing the machine. The word processor is the greatest revision tool in the history of writing. But you shouldn't be chained to it. The word processor is so efficient you can, assuming you type well, literally put down words as fast as they pop into your head. That can be incredibly useful when you're in the zone and incredibly dangerous when you're not. And it's never an ideal approach to proofreading. Proofreading demands a slow, careful pace. You need to be the tortoise, not the hare. Proofreading demands careful consideration of each word.

Proofreading is slow scrutiny. Take your time.

Find a comfortable chair. Turn off all distractions. Break out your red-ink pen. True, you will have to type all these changes into your word processing file later, but it's worth the added effort. When you work with pen and paper, you slow down. You catch things you would otherwise miss. Avoid potential embarrassments by being diligent.

Let me make another point about the proofreading process. Don't depend upon Spell-Check or, heaven forbid, Grammar Check. Rely upon Your-Brain-Check. I'm not saying you shouldn't pay attention to those red squiggly lines Spell-Check gives you. They may indicate a legitimate problem. Just don't imagine that's all there is to proofreading.

Remember, all Spell-Check does is ensure that the letters you've typed make a word. It has no idea if that's the right word or the word you intended. It just checks to see if it's a word—and it doesn't even do that flawlessly, as you may know if you have a strong vocabulary or use terms of art from a particular profession. You've heard the horror stories, like the author intending the heading on that page to be "Errata," but it gets published as "Erotica." Or "pubic" instead of "public." Taylor Mali has written a wonderful poem on this subject entitled "The Impotence of Proofreading" and the only thing better than reading it is hearing him perform it, in a video you can readily find on YouTube.

Don't let this happen to you. You have a miniature computer close at hand. You may call it a "smartphone," but it is in fact a computer more powerful than what NASA had when it put Neil Armstrong on the moon. With this incredibly advanced tool, you can look up words, spellings, and grammar rules, in about four seconds. When a tool that good is ubiquitous, there is simply no excuse for careless mistakes.

Grammar Check is better than it used to be, but it's far from foolproof. It particularly doesn't understand that on occasion fiction writers knowingly break the so-called rules. Like employing sentence fragments (which I just did). Or single-sentence paragraphs. Or having ignoramus characters say "ain't" or spew profanity.

Don't even get me started on Text Correct. Turn it off. Do you really want Siri rewriting (I have a friend who calls it "wrong-writing") your words? If you want vivid demonstrations of the horrors that could result from not proofing your texts or email, visit the website "Damn You AutoCorrect." Sadly, I know some people, particularly in the business world, who think proof-reading is of so little import that their mantra is "I do my best proofreading after I hit Send."

Careers have been made by well-written texts and email. Protect your reputation as a first-rate writer by producing error-free work wherever you are.

If you're concerned that editing with pen and paper will create more work or take too long, think of this instead as one more chance to go through your work and make sure it's as it should be. And if that doesn't work for you—hire someone to do the typing. And if you don't think you can justify that cost—get one of your kids to do it. Make them earn that allowance.

SPEAK TO ME WITH THINE OWN WORDS

THE THIRD PROOFREADING OPTION ON THE LIST IS READING YOUR work aloud. This is a procedure I have heard some people swear by and, again, this is something I would never do in a million years. Remember that the point of proofreading is not only to catch errors but also to improve your use of language. It is not meant to be fun. It is not meant to be entertaining. And it is not meant to give you another opportunity to revel in the magic of your prose, which I suspect is sometimes the true reason people read their words to themselves. You're not supposed to be rehearsing for your first book reading. You're supposed to be improving your work.

In his book on writing, David Morrill, a writer I respect enormously, argues strongly against reading your work aloud. His argument is that when you read work aloud, you can make it better than it actually is, subtly or subconsciously, by using vocal inflection, speeding or slowing your pace, perhaps even adding facial expressions. These are all ways of sweetening the text that do not exist on the printed page.

I agree with David. If all you're trying to find are typos, and you can't slow yourself down any other way, maybe reading aloud will help you catch a boo-boo or two. But it will never help you improve your work in any more profound way. Remember that your readers will not have the benefit of your vocal mastery. They must read it silently to themselves based upon what is actually on the page. Therefore, the only reliable way to review your work is to attempt to reproduce the experience of your future readers—by reading it silently to yourself, trying to forget all your insight into what's coming next. Reading it knowing only what has actually appeared on the page so far—and seeing if it works.

Review your work silently—as your future readers will.

Listen to Your Words

Just to totally confuse you, I'll mention here that I am a strong believer in listening to the sounds of your words—but you should be listening silently, not orating to yourself. As every great public speaker knows, sometimes the sound of words, the repetitions of phonemes, the skillful use of symmetry and pattern, can make a passage more memorable. If you take this too far, you've got one of those attention-getting darlings that may need to be cut. But if you do it right, you may have a gloriously memorable passage that people remember long after they've finished reading the book.

I'm not going to give a long lecture on rhetoric, but there are many so-called rhetorical devices that have proven to be excellent ways of giving your words some extra zing. There are literally dozens of them, but I've assembled a list of the most popular and the most effective and put it into Appendix D, along with some noteworthy examples of how they have been employed in the past.

Unless you have an incredibly intelligent, possibly pretentious, character, these probably shouldn't find their way into your dialogue. But they might work somewhere else. Think how much more memorable Dickens' great novel, *A Tale of Two Cities*, became simply because of the last passage: "It is a far far better thing I do than I have ever done. It is a far better rest I go to than I have ever known." Had this been in the middle of the book, it might have drawn too much attention to the author. But as a parting shot, the last supposed thoughts of the character about to make a noble sacrifice, it's perfect, and leaves every reader with a huge smile and a warm feeling for the whole human race.

In history class, when you studied the American Revolution, you probably read Thomas Paine, who rallied the support of the colonists with *The American Crisis*. Consider the memorable opening phrase from the book:

THESE ARE THE TIMES THAT TRY MEN'S SOULS.

LIKE THE FAMOUS WORDS OF NEIL ARMSTRONG WE CONSIDERED

before, this line has been artfully arranged to give it a power that goes beyond the mere meaning of the words. It has rhetorical force. It's memorable, in part due to the alliteration—the repeating initial "t" sound. Part of the magic is rhythmic—the line is almost perfect iambic pentameter, the rhythm of Shakespeare and many other great poets (we will forgive the one anapestic foot). There is consonance in the recurring "s" sound—"men's" and "souls." Plus it's simply a powerful way of expressing what Paine had to say, a feeling with which many colonists could sympathize.

I would be willing to bet this phrase did not emerge in Paine's first draft.

The first time through, he probably wrote something like: "Man, these are tough times!" Perhaps in the fourth or fifth draft, this was refined to: "How trying it is to live in times like these. On the soul, I mean." Or perhaps in the sixth draft: "Soulwise, these are trying times."

But eventually, because he wasn't satisfied with half-good or good enough, he stumbled upon his masterpiece. One we're still quoting two hundred and fifty years later.

The sounds and rhythm of your sentences can make them more memorable.

In Appendix E, I've assembled some of the most striking phrases from novels. None of these stop the plot dead in its tracks, but all of them improve their stories and make them unforgettable. None of them rose to the level of darlings that had to be exterminated. If there had been too many of them too close together, that might have happened. But as employed by skillful writers willing to revise and proof and refine their work, they memorably enhanced what was already on the page.

Learn to listen to your words. But listen silently. Read them as your reader will. Make the reading experience a pleasure.

. . .

OUTSOURCING THE EDITING

I HOPE YOU DETECTED THE SCORN IN MY EARLIER REFERENCE TO book doctors. I want you to learn to edit yourself. That said, I do think there are times when getting outside input can be valuable. Not as an excuse for avoiding work, but as a supplement, a chance to get an additional set of eyes that might see what you're missing.

I would never do this before you've got the book in what you think is final form, or darn close to it. But at the point when you think you've got your tale just about as good as it can possibly be, then you might consider shipping it out to trusted eyes. A professional editor might see a boo-boo you've missed. Or catch an incorrect fact or unintended anachronism. Sometimes we simply become too close to our own work to be objective.

The benefits of getting outside input can go beyond mere proofing. One of my favorite writers, Phillip Margolin, tells me that when he thinks he's finished a book, he sends it out to his Committee of Ten. These are his beta readers (I guess he's the alpha reader) who read the manuscript and give him feedback, what they liked and didn't like, what worked and what didn't. These are not just random readers. These are people he knows, people who are voracious readers, people whose opinions he respects.

You may be wondering, why so many? Is this a sign of deep-seated insecurity? Far from it. Phillip's theory is that if just one reader holds an opinion, it's an outlier, so he doesn't worry too much about it. Just one reader can't stand a character all the others loved? No worries. You're never gonna please everyone. But if five or six people voice the same complaint, it's time to sit up and listen. Even though no one wants to do major revisions when they think they're close to the finish line, you can't shirk the work, not if five out of ten hate a character, or six think the resolution is too coincidental, or four think the climax is disappointing.

When Phil gets the same thought from several people, he knows he has to take it seriously, even if he disagrees. Better to hear it from friends and fix it in advance than read about it all over your Amazon page in a long series of one-star reviews.

At the right time, seek reliable outside input.

This will not work if you resist outside input. You have to be willing to rethink anything and everything. Nothing is immune to change if it will improve your book. And you must be especially careful not to reject any suggestion out of hand. Even if it would be a lot of work, would this change make the book better? It doesn't matter if the character is secretly based upon you or your worst enemy and they would never do something like that. You want to write a sensational book. So listen to what people say. You don't have to implement every suggestion you hear. But you should always at least give it some thought.

HIGHLIGHTS/EXERCISES

Highlights

1) Proofreading matters.

2) The four most common proofreading techniques are: reading the manuscript backwards, reading the pages or sentences out of order, reading the manuscript aloud, and getting someone else to do it.

3) Review your work silently—as your future readers will.

4) The sounds and rhythm of your sentences can make them more memorable.

5) At the right time, seek reliable outside input.

Red Sneaker Exercises

1) When you have a manuscript you think is at the proofreading stage, try each of the methods discussed in this chapter. Can you

read the entire manuscript backward? If that proves too painful, try reading the pages in random order. Note that this will not help you fix story or character problems—but you should have already addressed those issues before you reached the proof-reading stage.

2) Try reading your manuscript word-for-word. I don't mean read it aloud, but read it silently, subvocalizing. I know you wouldn't actually do that if you were reading this for pleasure, but it may help you get a sense of how the words fit together to form sentences. Does it sound right? You might catch the frequent repetition or overuse of a particular word or phrase. Or you might spot some opportunities for creating a memorable or stylized phrasing.

3) Could you assemble a Committee of Ten? Do you know ten people you consider reliable readers? Ideally, they should be people who read the kind of work you're writing but are not necessarily writers themselves. Writers tend to be too conscious of style and structure and other technical aspects. You want someone who reads like a reader.

4) If you can't assemble a Committee of Ten, maybe you can start with a Committee of Five. Or even One. But make sure the One is someone you trust. Probably your reader should not be a spouse or close friend. Friends want you to be happy, which naturally inclines them to give positive feedback that might make you feel good about yourself but will not improve your book in the slightest. You want someone who will be honest, someone who will not hesitate to give you the down and dirty. They don't have to be mean about it. But they do have to be honest. The idea is to help you make the book better, and that may not happen, or their advice may be too easily dismissed, if they're not straight-forward.

5) Do you have a Facebook page? Odds are you're already active on some social media, and Facebook is by far the most popular, as well as the best for promoting books. Could you use a Facebook page to recruit beta readers? You may already post about the book you're writing, but even if you don't, this is a great chance to find out your friends' interests, who reads and who doesn't, and start building your Committee of Ten. And once your book is published, that Facebook page and those reading friends will be the foundation of your marketing plans.

7

WHEN AM I FINISHED?

"You write to communicate to the hearts and minds of others what's burning inside you, and we edit to let the fire show through the smoke."

— ARTHUR PLOTNIK

There remains one more step in the writing process that I haven't discussed, one that is just as important as the others. It may not be immediately obvious to you, and it may not be possible in all situations. In fact, you will probably have to make it possible.

Set it aside for a time.

Do you see now why I said this might not always be possible? If you're writing under time constraints, if you drive too close to the deadline, you may not have this luxury. But you should do it whenever possible. Because ultimately, your best editor will always be you. No one will ever know this book better. But the truth is, after all these drafts, perhaps ten or more by this point, you may have lost some objectivity. You may be too close to the source. If you can set it aside for a time, however, and then come back to it, you will regain that objectivity. You will be reading with some degree of freshness, seeing it as the non-author reader will.

Who knows what you might see.

THE BEAUTY OF TIME

PERHAPS SOME OF YOU WORK PUZZLES. I LOVE PUZZLES AND GAMES and anything else that challenges my brain in an entertaining way. So have you ever been in that situation where you've finished almost the entire crossword, but you can't figure what goes in one slot? It's all perfect—except what the blazes goes in that crossing between 4 Across and 8 Down? You stare at it and you think as hard as you can but you can't get it, so eventually you put the puzzle down and do something else. Perhaps you come back to it the next morning. Then you pick up the puzzle and look at it—

And the answer comes to you immediately.

What happened? How are you seeing what was impossible to see before? Part of it may be that you've rested. Your brain rebooted. But more importantly, the distance of time has allowed your brain to approach this problem from a fresh angle. Perhaps your subconscious has been working on the problem. Whatever the reason, you're looking at the problem with new eyes and you see potential problems you did not see before.

I recently had the value of time demonstrated to me in a powerful way. I'd written a novel titled *The Game Master* two years before, but for various complicated contractual reasons I won't bore you with, it wasn't immediately published. When it was finally scheduled, I pulled out the manuscript, not having looked at it in two years, and I thought…

Who wrote this mess? And why hasn't he read the Red Sneakers books?

Seriously. The passage of time gave me the ability to see the work objectively in a way that simply wasn't possible when I was in the process of working on it. I had other problems to solve at that time, making the plot work, making the characters shine, etc. But that left me blind to other issues that glared at me when I came back to it later.

Fortunately, I started plenty early and had lots of opportunities to fix the problems. As a result, I think *The Game Master* is one of my best, and certainly one of my most original, novels.

Time allowed me to make the book even better.

Give yourself the benefit of time.

If you get nothing else from this discussion, I hope you grasp this: a deadline is no excuse for turning in second-rate work. Start early enough to do the job properly and go through all the steps in the writing process. If you don't have a deadline, put the manuscript aside for a while after you think it's finished. A month is good, but even a week is better than nothing. When you return to your work, you'll be glad you did this. You'll see a way to make it even better than it already is. Be grateful that you have this time to make improvements. The great writer Alexander Pope, all those centuries ago, wrote, "Compose with fury and revise with phlegm."

But I like the way Ray Bradbury said it best: "Writing has two parts. Throwing up and cleaning up."

Well, this is the last stage of the cleanup. If you've taken your time and worked through all the steps, you're looking at a novel that sparkles like a diamond. How can you look at that without feeling enormous pride?

FORMATTING

.   .   .

Now that your book is ready you want to start marketing it, and that means it needs to be formatted correctly. I've seen a lot of bad information floating around on this subject, so let me briefly tell you how professional manuscripts are formatted today (even when they will be submitted electronically). Set this up as default settings on your word processor, save it, and you won't have to worry about it again.

1. Times New Roman, 12 pt. font, black ink. (Don't ever let anyone suggest you can "attract more attention" by doing something different, like a fancy cursive font or pink ink. You will just look like an amateur.)
2. One-inch margins on all four sides
3. Header in the upper right corner of every page containing the title or a significant word from the title followed by the page number, i.e., Editing-12
4. Double-space throughout
5. Left-justify the text.
6. Biographical and contact information should be on a separate page because in some instances the manuscript will be read "blind," that is, by people who don't want to know who you are as they read it.
7. One space between sentences, not two. If you're in the habit of typing two spaces, no problem. After you're finished, use Find and Replace to change all the two-spaces to one-spaces.
8. Indent paragraphs a half-inch.
9. Eliminate Tab Characters. Why? Because they complicate converting the manuscript to an eBook file. Set your computer to automatically indent paragraphs when you hit the Return key. If you haven't done this, though, you can always remove those Tab Characters with Find and Replace.

10. Indicate scene breaks within chapters with a single pound sign (what tweeters call a hashtag) between the scenes. Your publisher will leave this space blank or convert it to something else, but the pound sign will ensure the scenes remain separated. Don't center the pound sign (or anything else) by pushing it across with the space bar. Use the Center Justify tool.

YES, THAT'S NICE—BUT WHEN AM I FINISHED?

I UNDERSTAND THE DESIRE TO COMPLETE THE NOVEL AND MOVE ON to something else. That's inevitable any time you tackle a large task. And at this point, your book is probably so fantastic—and you know it is—that you're anxious for people to see it. So when can others have the pleasure of enjoying this masterwork? When can you take it out on the road and show it around?

This is a difficult question to answer with any response that you will find remotely satisfying. Because the best answer I can give is: When it's ready to go, you'll know.

This is not intended to give you excuses for skipping steps in the writing process. Resist the temptation, halfway through the revision stage, to think, "Ah, well, the brilliance of the prose will compensate for any minor errors." Or anything like that. If you want to play in the big leagues, you have to do major league work.

If you've been through all the steps in this process, including giving yourself the benefit of time and sober second thoughts, you're probably feeling pretty darn good about this book. And deservedly so.

You'll know when it's time to stop working on the first book—and start working on the second.

Perhaps you've heard the famous quote from Gene Fowler: "A book is never finished; it's abandoned." There is some truth in that, but it doesn't mean you should quit before you've completed the process. I think it simply recognizes that if I set *The Game Master* aside for another two years, I might well find something else to change. But at some point you have to let it go or you've defeated the main purpose, which is to have other people read it. If you've seriously and purposefully worked through the steps in this process, which took some considerable time, then you should feel no embarrassment about setting your work loose upon the world.

And then you start your next book.

I wish I could guarantee you will sell your first book. I can't. Even if it turns out spectacularly well, there is no assurance it will be published. I was exceedingly fortunate and managed to publish my first book, but I know many better writers who did not. Success in the arts is a combination of many factors, and the quality of the work is only one of them.

Here's the only thing I can guarantee. If you keep working, keep pushing through all the steps in the writing process and giving it your maximum daily effort, eventually you will have the right book in the right place at the right time. That's when you get published. I can't tell you *when* it will happen, but I can tell you unequivocally that it *will* happen.

Unless you quit.

Never give up.

Where Do I Go From Here?

Presumably, you are now going to take your work out to see if you can get it published. This is not arrogance on your part. This is a privilege you have earned by merit of your hard work. So be bold. Feel no insecurity. Go forth and sell that baby.

The publishing world has changed so dramatically that I feel any detailed comments on this subject will only date the book. Suffice to say, writers today have more options than they once did, and that's a good thing. Speaking as someone who has had numerous books published by large New York publishers, I can tell you that there are many advantages and disadvantages to this path. You have a huge network of professionals behind you, and that's great. But that network is going to keep the lion's share of the profits, and that's considerably less great. Add in the fact that you probably can't get that publisher without enlisting the aid of a literary agent, who will likely take 15-20% of the thin percent assigned to you, and you have a situation that is even less great.

Anything that puts more power in the hands of authors is, in my opinion, a good development. Traditionally, even though authors are theoretically the most irreplaceable player in the publishing process, the originators and creative sparks without whom publishing would not exist, they have not been compensated or treated as if they were the most important players in the chain. In the twenty-first century, creators should be more than cogs providing software for multinational corporations. So you should consider all your options.

There are many paths to publication.

This pertains to far more than money. Authors, like all artists, should have control over their creative output. But they don't, and ironically, in many cases, the more successful writers become, the less control they have. If you have a hit, the publisher will want more books like that one, and they will continue to want more books like that one until finally your readers are sick of it, at which time the publisher will dump you and find someone else. I've talked to more than one successful author who decided to start self-publishing to maintain control over his own career. At some point the artist gets tired of running to New York to ask for permission to write what he or she wants to write. Why does New York have veto power? Aren't I too old to still be asking Dad if I can borrow the car keys?

This has given rise to the self-publishing movement.

Self-publishing has always existed, in part because the large publishers weren't taking anywhere near all the people who wanted to write. But prior to the advent of eBooks, there was no mechanism for making self-publishing a successful venture. You couldn't get your books into stores, it cost too much to print them, and they all ended up collecting dust in the garage. Self-publishing had few success stories, and the few that existed generally involved savvy promoters attracting enough attention through relentless hand-marketing to eventually obtain the attention of a major publisher.

EBooks changed that. Now there are writers leading successful careers, both financially and creatively, by publishing themselves, or in some cases leading "hybrid" careers, self-publishing some work and licensing others to publishing houses. Why does this work? Because all the major costs of publishing—printing, distributing, shipping, warehousing—don't exist for eBooks. Those costs were the usual corporate explanation for why writers received such a slim percentage of the profits. None of them are relevant to eBooks, but even after the eBook revolution, publishers were reluctant to alter their royalty split. As of this writing, those percentages have changed precious little. For people who have the entrepreneurial spirit, who like being in charge of their own destiny, self-publishing is a course to consider.

Ebooks have dramatically changed the publishing industry.

You may think self-publishing will involve a lot of marketing effort and time spent on social media. But the truth is, you will need to do that no matter what publishing path you pursue.

You will have to participate in the marketing and publicity of your book.

Let me make two things clear. First, I am not pushing self-publishing or suggesting that it is superior. I'm glad authors have options. But which option you pursue is a decision only you can make. Second, the most important factor you should consider is: What will make me happy as a writer? What would I consider success? What would make me feel justified in having spent so much time writing this book?

Let me describe the two paths. Then you decide for yourself. Am I going to start looking for an agent? Or am I going to start educating myself about self-publishing?

If you pursue traditional publishing, you must:

- Get an agent
- Accept a royalty rate between 4-15% (maybe a bit better for eBooks)
- Live with someone else formatting, designing, marketing, and distributing your book
- Actively market your book

AND THESE ARE THE PLUSSES AND MINUSES:

- **Pros**: The publisher takes the risks and bears the costs
- You have professionals working on your book at all stages
- You have few upfront costs and better distribution (in bookstores)
- You may have greater unit sales
- You can tell your friends you have a big-time publisher

- **Cons**: You have little control over the process
- You give away your rights, which you will probably never get back
- You still have to market extensively
- The unit price will be relatively high
- You wait a long time to be paid
- Your royalty rate will be much smaller

TRADITIONAL PUBLISHING HAS MANY ADVANTAGES AND **disadvantages.**

What about the self-publishing or hybrid route? What should I expect there? You should expect to:

- Hire an editor
- Learn book formatting
- Learn about distribution
- Learn about design
- Master marketing and publicity
- Consider eBook, print-on-demand, and audiobook options

AND THE PLUSES AND MINUSES?

- **Pros**: You control every step of the process
- You retain your rights
- You can publish or change your book at will
- You can leave books in print forever
- You can choose your price and pulse price

- You can get your work to readers faster and more frequently
- You are paid almost immediately
- You have a much higher royalty rate per unit
- If there's something you can't learn to do or don't want to do, you can hire someone to do it for you
- **Cons**: There's a high learning curve
- Like running any business, it's a lot of work
- There will be some upfront costs
- You will still have to do lots of marketing if you hope to sell books
- Even if you master the learning curve, you will still have to pay for some services, such as cover design (and an amateurish cover will doom your book)

SELF-PUBLISHING HAS MANY ADVANTAGES AND DISADVANTAGES.

Ten years ago I would've advised all my students to avoid self-publishing, which seemed a complete waste of time, and in some cases, a form of giving up. But now the world has changed. I have seen people make this choice for a variety of reasons—their age, their personality and temperament, their marketing savvy—and they made it work.

Choose the path to publication that's the best fit for you.

If you follow all the steps in the writing process, you will have a first-rate book, which is what's most important. Your validation should come from the fact that you did good work, not that it was signed off on by some corporation that thought it could make money off your efforts. The happy fact is, the better your book, the more doors will open. And this will happen because you put in the work, because you went through all the steps in the writing process.

Because you edited with excellence.

Your reader may simply find this an entertaining way to pass some time, but you know that nothing good comes easy. You can be proud of the effort that went into entertaining that reader. You can be proud that you made your dream come true.

You're a first-rate writer now. The possibilities are endless.

HIGHLIGHTS/EXERCISES

Highlights

1) Set it aside for a time.

2) Give yourself the benefit of time.

3) You'll know when it's time to stop working on the first book—and start working on the second.

4) Never give up.

5) There are many paths to publication.

6) Ebooks have dramatically changed the publishing industry.

7) If you want to be successful, you will have to participate in the marketing and publicity of your book.

8) Traditional publishing has many advantages and disadvantages.

9) Self-publishing has many advantages and disadvantages.

10) Choose the path to publication that's the best fit for you.

Red Sneaker Exercises

1) When you write your first draft, try to follow the Writer's Calendar in Appendix A. When you write the subsequent drafts, keep your own calendar. Notice how long each revision takes. Assuming you work regularly, you should see each subsequent draft take a little less time. When you think you're done, calendar yourself a month away from the manuscript (perhaps planning your next one), then give it another read. Did you find a need for revision that wasn't apparent before?

2) How much time do you spend on social media? Odds are you have a Facebook page and have tweeted at least once in your life. If you're under forty, you're probably even more active. Social media is the primary means by which books are marketed today. Statistically speaking, over 70% of all internet-active adults—and 10% of all people on Earth—have a Facebook page. It has become the most cost-effective way to promote books, and one that has been astoundingly successful for those who use it well. Whether you find a publisher or publish yourself, you will likely have to participate. Even before your book is out, you should 1) attach a signature block with contact information to all your email, 2) reserve a domain name, preferably your-writer-name.com, 3) create an Amazon author page, and 4) create two Facebook pages, one for friends and one for fans. Be confident. You will have fans at some point.

3) Give some serious thought to how you would like to be published. Try to make your decision based upon solid informa-tion, not snob appeal, or the desire to impress your acquain-

tances, or the need for personal validation. Validation should come from the fact that you worked through all the steps in the writing process and completed a first-rate book, not that it was acquired by a large multinational corporation. I don't want to disillusion you, but corporations exist for only one reason, and it is not to promote the arts. A book contract means the powers-that-be believe they can make money by publishing your book, not that they think it has artistic merit. I hope it also means they love your writing, but given some of the stuff I see published, I'm forced to conclude that is not necessarily so. The factors you should consider are: 1) your motivations for writing, 2) how long you're willing to wait, and 3) whether you want to become a small-businessperson. It has more to do with temperament than talent. Which path is right for you?

APPENDIX A: WRITER'S CALENDAR

Is it possible to finish a top-quality manuscript in six months? Of course it is, if you're willing to do the work necessary to make it happen. Here's how:

Week 1

Commit to your writing schedule.

Find your writing place.

Inform friends and family that you are undertaking a major project and you would like their support.

Consider what you want to write. Start thinking like a writer.

Week 2

Commit to a premise—then make it bigger. Is it big and unique enough to attract a publisher?

Commit to a genre. What's your spin on the genre? How will you make it the same—but different? Research as needed.

Week 3

Develop your main protagonist and antagonist.

What are their best qualities—and worst? What drives them?

What is your protagonist's character arc? What does he/she want, seek, desire?

Write a half-page example of dialogue for each major character in their distinct voice.

Week 4

Put all major events (scenes) on index cards, approximately sixty total.

Arrange cards by acts. Highlight the Plot Turning Points and Character Turning Points.

Type the index cards into an outline, adding detail when you have it.

Week 5

Think about the shape of your story—the Plot. Will your character experience positive growth or maturation? Redemption? Disillusionment?

Map out twists and turns to maintain reader interest. What is the last twist the reader will suspect?

Don't shy away from a great scene because it doesn't fit your story as you currently understand it. See if you can change the story to accommodate the great scene.

Weeks 6-18

Write at least five pages every day—ten on Saturdays. No editing. Just keep moving ahead.

Do additional writing as necessary to complete 10 % of the book each week.

Week 19-23

Perform triage on what you've written. Revise. Then revise more. Focus on character consistency, character depth. Are the characters sympathetic or empathetic?

Focus on plot, pacing, story logic, theme. Is the story plausible?

Week 24-26

Give the manuscript to trusted reader(s).

Obtain comments from readers. Incorporate comments from readers where appropriate.

Set it aside for a time, then reread it with fresh eyes. Do you see problems you didn't spot before?

And then—

Attend writing conferences and bounce your ideas off agents and editors. If people don't ask to see your manuscript, your premise needs work. If people ask to see pages but don't take you on, it suggests your manuscript is not yet ready. Consider attending a small-group writing retreat to give your book that final push it needs to be publishable.

APPENDIX B: SEARCH AND DESTROY LIST

1. pretty
2. very
3. started to
4. began to
5. There were
6. It was
7. ! (One per manuscript)
8. almost
9. maybe
10. perhaps
11. noticed
12. wondered
13. just
14. guessed
15. really
16. suddenly
17. knew
18. kind of

19. tried
20. all
21. thing(s)
22. stuff
23. is, are
24. was, were
25. that
26. -ing verbs (especially if starting a sentence or used with a helping verb)
27. numerals (always write out numbers unless the number is so large it's impractical
28. ; (Why?)
29. and (in compound sentences – break them up into separate sentences)
30. have, had (avoid if at all possible)
31. Finger quotes (if you mean "so-called" then write "so-called" but avoid snicker quotes)

APPENDIX C: STYLE TIPS

1. Avoid weak openings, such as "Pronoun Followed by To-Be Verb," as in "It is" and "There are" and They are." Instead, use definite subjects and strong action verbs that bring energy and precision to your sentence. You can usually fix sentences that start this way by inverting them, that is, by converting the object into the subject.

2. Avoid to-be verbs whenever possible. Instead of using them as helping verbs, change the tense of the verb and ditch the helper.

3. Avoid phrasal verbs, such as "stand up" and "carry on." There's usually a more succinct and more powerful single-word replacement.

4. Eliminate unnecessary words. The longer the sentence, the more difficult it is for a reader to absorb. Many words before the subject, or between the subject and the verb, or between the verb and the object, will make the sentence more difficult to follow.

5. Work to find the precise word to say exactly what you want to say in the strongest possible way. Twain: "The

difference between the almost-right word and the right word is the difference between the lightning bug and the lightning."

6. Eliminate redundancy.

7. Avoid word repetition, particularly noticeable words repeating in the same sentence.

8. Eliminate embarrassing grammar errors such as subject-verb agreement problems. If you're unsure about a rule, look it up.

9. Avoid clichés. Invent fresh and original ways of expressing your thoughts.

10. Eliminate run-on sentences, fragments, and comma splices.

11. Don't risk misspellings that erode confidence. Use a dictionary app to your advantage.

12. If you are tempted to use an adverb, choose a stronger verb instead. Avoid all degree adverbs, such as "very" and "really" and "pretty."

13. Use the Oxford comma.

14. The titles of short works should be put in quotation marks. The titles of long works should be italicized.

15. Punctuation marks should be placed inside the quotation marks.

16. Avoid prepositional phrases and other unnecessary words that clutter and complicate your sentences.

17. Jefferson: "The greatest of virtues is that of never using two words where one will do." If a word doesn't contribute anything to your sentence, remove it.

18. Multiple-word adjectives (phrasal adjectives) should be hyphenated, as in "multiple-word adjectives."

19. Avoid passive voice, unless you're using it for a specific strategic reason. Active voice will give your sentences more immediacy and power.

APPENDIX D: FIFTH DRAFT CHECKLIST

Is there a reason to care about these characters?

Does the motivation deepen as the story progresses? Do the stakes increase?

Is there tension on every page? Does the tension start with the first sentence?

Are descriptive details and dialogue voice unique to each major character?

Are there too many similar scenes in a row?

Does the pace slow at any point?

How many emotional triggers have you put into place? How will they affect the reader?

Does your protagonist demonstrate a sympathetic or empathetic quality in the first five pages?

Do the plot complications increase as the story progresses?

What is extraordinary about this character or world or plot you've created?

Have you said what you wanted to say with this story?

APPENDIX E: GREAT LINES FROM GREAT BOOKS

APPENDIX E: GREAT LINES FROM GREAT BOOKS

It was the best of times, it was the worst of times, it was the age of wisdom, it was the age of foolishness, it was the epoch of belief, it was the epoch of incredulity, it was the season of Light, it was the season of Darkness, it was the spring of hope, it was the winter of despair, we had everything before us, we had nothing before us, we were all going direct to Heaven, we were all going direct the other way – in short, the period was so far like the present period, that some of its noisiest authorities insisted on its being received, for good or for evil, in the superlative degree of comparison only. —Charles Dickens, *A Tale of Two Cities*

Fate is like a strange, unpopular restaurant, filled with odd waiters who bring you things you never asked for and don't always like. —Lemony Snicket

Life isn't about what happens to you, it's about how you handle what happens. —Nicholas Evans, *The Smoke Jumper*

Death is but the next great adventure. —Albus Dumbledore (J.K. Rowling) (*Harry Potter and the Sorcerer's Stone*)

And I, of course, am innocent of all but malice. —Fiona, *Sign of the Unicorn*, Roger Zelazny

And if you're going to criticize me for not finishing the whole thing and tying it up in a bow for you, why, do us both a favor and write your own damn book, only have the decency to call it a romance instead of a history, because history's got no bows on it, only frayed ends of ribbons and knots that can't be untied. It ain't a pretty package, but then it's not your birthday that I know of so I'm under no obligation to give you a gift. —Orson Scott Card, *Alvin Journeyman*

Because we are the people, and the people go on. —Ma Joad, *The Grapes of Wrath*, John Steinbeck

Death belongs to God alone. By what right do men touch that unknown thing? —Victor Hugo, *Les Misérables*

Life is a Gift Horse. —J.D. Salinger, *Teddy*

Life is pain. Anybody that says different is selling something. —Fezzik's mother, *The Princess Bride*

Not all who wander are lost. —J.R.R. Tolkien, *The Fellowship of the Ring*

The surest sign that there is intelligent life elsewhere in the universe is that none of it has tried to contact us. —*Calvin and Hobbes*

A bore is a person who deprives you of solitude without

providing you with company. —John MacDonald, *The Turquoise Lament*

All animals are equal, but some are more equal than others. —George Orwell, *Animal Farm*

Behind them lay pain, and death, and fear. Ahead of them lay doubt, and danger, and fathomless mysteries. But they weren't alone. —Philip Pullman, *The Golden Compass*

Certain things should just stay as they are. You ought to be able to stick them in one of those big glass cases and just leave them alone. —JD Salinger, *Catcher in the Rye*

Dad, how do soldiers killing each other solve the world's problems? —*Calvin and Hobbes*

APPENDIX F: USEFUL RHETORICAL
DEVICES

APPENDIX F: USEFUL RHETORICAL DEVICES

- Use words and phrases skillfully to make your words more powerful and persuasive
- Rhetorical devices often create patterns of expectations that give power to your message.
- When you use rhetorical devices skillfully, often not only the meaning of your words but the sounds of your words become important.

Parallelism

- **Parallelism** involves the expression of similar ideas with similar patterns
- "…a struggle against the common enemies of man: tyranny, poverty, disease, and war itself." JFK
- "Let every nation know, whether it wishes us well or ill, that we shall **pay any price, bear any burden, meet any hardship, support any friend, oppose any foe** to assure the survival and the success of liberty." JFK

The Placement of Words and Clauses

- In **antimetabole**, a word or words at the end of a clause are repeated at the beginning of the next.
- "Let us never negotiate out of fear, but let us never fear to negotiate." JFK
- In **epanalepsis**, the initial words or words at the beginning of a clause or sentence are repeated at the end.
- "Mankind must put an end to war, or war will put an end to us." JFK
- In **anadiplosis**, the word or words at the end of a clause are repeated at the start of the next.
- "In the beginning was the Word, and the Word was God, and the Word was made God." KJV
- **Isocolon**: Using multiple clauses of similar length for rhetorical effect
- "The bigger they are, the harder they fall."
- "Let us preach what we practice, and practice what we preach." Churchill
- "People the world over have always been more impressed by the power of our example than by the example of our power." Bill Clinton
- "We were elected to change Washington, and we let Washington change us." John McCain
- **Anaphora**: repetition of a word or words at the beginning of successive clauses or sentences
- "Of all the gin joints in all the towns in all the world, she walks into mine." *Casablanca*
- **Polyptoton**: Repeating words with the same root, which allows the writer to maintain the emphasis without falling into a sing-song rhythm
- "…not as a call to bear arms, though arms we need, not as a call to battle, though embattled we are…" JFK

- "Absolute power corrupts absolutely." Lord Acton
- In **asyndeton**, you omit the usual conjunctions (connectors)
- "I came, I saw, I conquered." Julius Caesar
- "...that we shall pay any price, bear any burden, meet any hardship, support any friend, **oppose any foe** to assure the survival and the success of liberty." JFK
- In **polysyndeton**, you put in more conjunctions (connectors) than are necessary
- "...and that government of the people, by the people, **for the people** shall not perish from the earth" Lincoln
- In **hendiadys**: words are joined by a conjunction instead of a word and its modifier
- The weather is pleasant and warm. (instead of "pleasantly warm"

ABOUT THE AUTHOR

William Bernhardt is the author of forty-nine books, including *The Last Chance Lawyer (#1 Bestseller)*, the historical novels *Challengers of the Dust* and *Nemesis*, two books of poetry, and the Red Sneaker books on fiction writing. In addition, Bernhardt founded the Red Sneaker Writers Center to mentor aspiring author. The Center hosts an annual conference (WriterCon), small-group seminars, a newsletter, a phone app, and a bi-weekly podcast. He is also the owner of Balkan Press, which publishes poetry and fiction as well as the literary journal *Conclave*.

Bernhardt has received the Southern Writers Guild's Gold Medal Award, the Royden B. Davis Distinguished Author Award (University of Pennsylvania) and the H. Louise Cobb Distinguished Author Award (Oklahoma State), which is given "in recognition of an outstanding body of work that has profoundly influenced the way in which we understand ourselves and American society at large." In 2019, he received the Arrell Gibson Lifetime Achievement Award from the Oklahoma Center for the Book.

In addition Bernhardt has written plays, a musical (book and score), humor, children stories, biography, and puzzles. He has edited two anthologies (*Legal Briefs* and *Natural Suspect*) as fundraisers for The Nature Conservancy and the Children's Legal Defense Fund. In his spare time, he has enjoyed surfing, digging for dinosaurs, trekking through the Himalayas, paragliding, scuba diving, caving, zip-lining over the canopy of the Costa Rican rain forest, and jumping out of an airplane at 10,000 feet.

In 2017, when Bernhardt delivered the keynote address at the

San Francisco Writers Conference, chairman Michael Larsen noted that in addition to penning novels, Bernhardt can "write a sonnet, play a sonata, plant a garden, try a lawsuit, teach a class, cook a gourmet meal, beat you at Scrabble, and work the *New York Times* crossword in under five minutes."

For more information
www.williambernhardt.com
wb@williambernhardt.com

AUTHOR'S NOTE

Watch for the next volume in the Red Sneaker Writers Book series.

Would you consider posting a review of this book online? I'd really appreciate it. I hope you'll also consider reading some of my fiction, including the Daniel Pike novels, starting with *The Last Chance Lawyer*.

Please consider attending WriterCon over Labor Day weekend in Oklahoma City. For more information, visit www.writercon.org. If you're interested in attending one of my small-group writing retreats, visit my webpage.

Need some feedback on your writing? Check out my Patreon page at https://www.patreon.com/willbern

I publish a free e-newsletter on a regular basis. The Red Sneaker Writers Newsletter is for writers and aspiring writers, filled with market and writing news. You can sign up at my website. There's also a bi-weekly Red Sneakers podcast, available everywhere you get podcasts.

For more information, please visit my website at http://www.williambernhardt.com. You can email me at willbern@gmail.com.

Made in the USA
Columbia, SC
19 August 2024

40793531R00074